ROOKIE REINER

How to Survive and Thrive in the Show Pen

HEATHER COOK

T
TRAFALGAR SQUARE
NORTH POMFRET, VERMONT

First published in 2009 by
Trafalgar Square Books
North Pomfret, Vermont 05053

Printed in China

Library of Congress Cataloging-in-Publication Data

Cook, Heather, 1977-.
  Rookie reiner : how to survive and thrive in the show pen / Heather Cook.
    p. cm.
  Includes index.
  ISBN 978-1-57076-414-1
  1. Reining (Horsemanship) I. Title.
  SF296.R4C66 2009
  798.2'4--dc22

                                            2009035511

Book design by Carrie Fradkin
Typefaces: Rotis Serif, Scala Sans
10 9 8 7 6 5 4 3 2 1

Dedication

To Geri Greenall, who said I should. To Jodie Hines who said I could. And to my husband Randall Cook who always knew I would. Thank you.

Thank you to my Heavenly Father.

> *But those who hope in the Lord will renew their strength. They will soar on wings like eagles; they will run and not grow weary, they will walk and not grow faint."*
>
> *Isaiah 40:31*

Contents

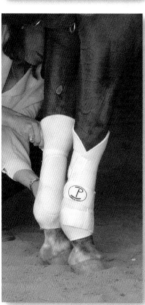

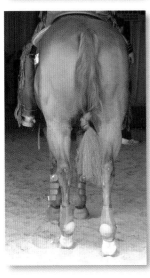

1 Introduction to Reining

Have you been looking for a sport that encourages a respectful, willing partnership between horse and human? If so, you've picked up the right book.

Reining is a relatively new discipline when you consider the length of time that people have been training horses for industry and sport, but its history runs deep. Its emergence came in the early 1960s just at the tail end of the real Western lifestyle where many Americans were still working ranches that their families had owned for generations. The horses they used for herding cattle and wrangling strays are the great-granddaddies of today's reining horses. The training techniques used to develop the maneuvers you'll find discussed in this book have actually been around for centuries, combining influences of dressage, roping, ranch work, racing, and even Spanish war horses.

The specialized reining maneuvers are derived from natural movements a horse performs when working cattle on a ranch. The better the horse, the more effectively a cowboy could do his job. In the late-nineteenth and early-twentieth centuries, a cowboy needed to sort, brand, doctor, or settle the cattle in his charge without the luxury of fencing. No one wanted to spend his days riding a horse that let a cow get away from him or one that took an acre to turn around, so a horse that could outrun a herd, catch up to and turn back a stray, react quickly, and perform well at a variety of speeds was valued above all—even more so, if the horse came with a good attitude and was a pleasure to ride.

WHAT IS A REINING HORSE?

Today, the reining horse has become known as an athlete. The National Reining Horse Association (NRHA) defines reining in a section of its handbook referred to as "A: General," and this text is most often quoted when you ask "What is a reining horse?" NRHA Hall of Famer, Jim Willoughby, wrote the following paragraph (taken from the 2009 *NRHA Handbook*) in 1966, and it has defined the reining horse ever since:

To rein a horse is not only to guide him, but also to control his every movement. The best reined horse should be willingly guided or controlled with little or no apparent resistance and dictated to completely. Any movement on his own must be considered a lack of control. All deviations from the exact written pattern must be considered a lack of/or temporary loss of control and therefore a fault that must be marked down according to severity of deviation. After deducting all faults,

The National Reining Horse Association

In 1966, the National Reining Horse Association (NRHA) was formed to promote the reining horse in the United States. Its objectives are: "To promote and encourage development of and public interest in agriculture and ranching through the promotion of public Reining Horse Shows; the development of suitable and proper standards of performance and judging intended to govern all Reining Horse Contests sponsored and approved by the National Reining Horse Association; to encourage the development and breeding of better Reining Horses; and to develop and disseminate informational material deemed desirable to provide contestants and spectators a better understanding of a proper performance of the Reining Horse in the show arena."

The NRHA is responsible for approving and regulating all reining horse shows in the world that use NRHA judges. Prior to the expansion of the sport into the international limelight, the NRHA developed the rulebook and judging system that the world reining bodies use today.

The growth of the NRHA has been on a steady increase over the past 15 years. From 1997 to 2007, the NRHA grew by over 40 percent to over 15,000 members; and from 265 NRHA-approved shows to 700. In 1997, a total of 1.3 million dollars was paid out in NRHA competition; and in 2006 the NRHA awarded over 10 million dollars in competition purses.

There are clubs all around the world that hold NRHA-sanctioned events each year. They are known as "affiliates" of the NRHA and pay an annual $100 fee to the NRHA. Each country may have a governing body of reining in their nation and may become an international affiliate. They are entitled to certain benefits and rebates from the NRHA and are charged with promoting the sport on behalf of their nationals (see Appendix, p. 132).

set here within, against execution of the pattern and the horse's overall performance, credit should be given for smoothness, finesse, attitude, quickness, and authority of performing various maneuvers, while using controlled speed, which raises the difficulty level and makes him more exciting and pleasing to watch to an audience.

BEGINNER-FRIENDLY

The sport of reining is most appropriate for beginning riders because the entire purpose of reining is to seek to control a horse while developing a willing partnership. Both rider and horse are taught cues that help them communicate with each other. Older, well-trained reining horses are often referred to as "push-button" horses because they have been taught distinct cues for each maneuver. If you can learn a reining horse's "buttons," you can learn how to ride him!

For example, reining horses are very often taught the word "Whoa" on the first or second day of their riding lives. Unequivocally it means "stop." Even the most green riders can bring their trained reining horse to a stop by using the word "Whoa."

Intermediate riders also find that reining helps them to develop better horsemanship and communication with their horse. By teaching the maneuvers they will often find he becomes a more willing participant in daily rides.

In addition to beginners and intermediate riders, experienced horsemen are also taking up reining for competition. It has a high appeal to these individuals because they can use their riding ability and apply it to an entirely new set of movements that are exciting and fun to perform. Reining's focus on horsemanship appeals as a way to further demonstrate the almost invisible connection that true horsemen have with a horse.

THE COMPETITION

Reining competitions are comprised of sets of classes, and riders enter a class based on criteria such as their ability level and/or experience, or the amount of money already earned by horse or rider (see more on this, p. 87. Each horse and rider combination gets to compete once in each class and this is called their "run."

1.1 *A circling horse demonstrates his ability to be guided by the rider at different speeds. The reining horse is required to circle at both a gallop and a controlled lope in both directions.*

One pattern is chosen for each class and every combination completes—and is judged on—its performance of that pattern. A pattern is a set of defined maneuvers completed in a specific order (see chapter 11, p. 76).

The patterns are determined ahead of time and posted so that riders know which pattern is required. Most of the time, they are chosen from a specific set of patterns designed by the NRHA. However, there are other associations with their own patterns that I will discuss later.

Maneuvers

Before we go any further, let's define all the maneu-vers you will find in a reining pattern and why they are there. Later, I'll discuss each maneuver individually (see p. 67), as well as outline the athletic qualities required of the horse and describe rider physiology.

Circle: There are two types of circles called for in a reining pattern—the "large fast" and the "small slow" (fig. 1.1). These two maneuvers are exactly what they say: one is a large circle performed at a fast pace (a gallop), the other a small one and performed slowly (at a controlled lope). They always appear in the same ratio of two to one: two large fast circles to one small slow circle. The circle maneuvers demonstrate that a horse is able to be moved from a large circle down into a

1.2 The lead change demonstrates a horse's ability to perform exact maneuvers on cue. Here the rider gives the cue for the left lead departure.

smaller circle without leaning in, pulling on the reins, or fighting the change, and that this transition is completed in a willing fashion.

Lead Change: There is only one type of lead change in reining, the flying change (fig. 1.2). This maneuver requires your horse to switch leads while changing direction at the center of the arena, commonly referred to as "X." The horse must change leads on both the front and hind legs in the same stride; you are penalized if your horse changes late or early, or if he changes the front or the hind feet only.

Spin: The spin calls for the horse to "plant" his inside hind leg in the ground and rotate his entire body around that point (fig. 1.3). His other hind leg helps to balance him, and moves around the planted inside hind. The front legs provide the impulsion. For this maneuver to be performed correctly, the inside front leg must reach sideways and pull the horse toward it, then the outside front leg must step across the inside front. The turn must be cadenced (have a steady rhythm) and be performed with speed.

Stop: The hallmark of the reining horse is his sliding stop (fig. 1.4). To stop correctly, a horse must first be running at speed. His hind legs push forward into the ground, and specially designed horse shoes called "sliding plates," or "sliders," allow the hind feet to slide along the surface. His front feet alternately step forward in a motion referred to as "pedaling" and should not brace or stop the forward momentum.

Rollback: A rollback is executed after a horse has come to a stop (fig. 1.5). It can also be referred to as a "rollback over the haunches." The horse keeps his hind feet in place, elevates his shoulders, and turns. It is almost like a 180-degree spin rotation, but the horse must come out of the rollback at a lope. If he trots out of the rollback, he is penalized.

Back-Up: The back-up is best performed when the horse moves freely in reverse with little or no apparent resistance (fig. 1.6). Some horses are more athletic and can move backward quite quickly. A resistant horse may "push" on the bit or swish his tail.

Some breeds excel at reining because they have the body structure that lets them perform the maneuvers more easily than others. This does not mean that certain breeds cannot do them, just that some are better at it and will be more successful in the show arena. I discuss these maneuvers in greater detail in chapter 10 (see p. 67), and breeds best for reining in chapter 3 (p. 17).

1.3 The spin is a specialized reining move that requires incredible athleticism. The horse must rotate his entire body around his inside hind leg in a cadenced and quick manner.

REINING ORGANIZATIONS

When you first begin to compete, you have many different choices depending on your level of experience, your horse's experience, the amount of money you may have won in other sports, or your lack of all three. Many horses come to reining—and riders—from other disciplines (something I discuss in chapter 9, p. 59).

There are different organizations that can meet your needs based on where you are going to show. Some require memberships, others do not. In upcoming chapters I describe in detail how and where to start showing, but as an introduction to the sport, I'm including some basic information here.

This list of places to compete is in order of the least competitive to most. As you and your horse improve, where you show will change.

Open Club Shows

These shows are called "open club" because they are open to any competitor. The clubs that host and run the shows are not normally membership-based and serve a relatively small, regional population of riders. An open club show may include classes in everything from "hunter hack" to "showmanship" to "reining." The club may have developed its own rulebook, be run out of someone's kitchen, only give away ribbons recycled

1.4 *A sliding stop is an identifying move for a reining horse and can be the hardest maneuver to learn. The front feet continue forward motion as the hind slide along the surface of the ground to the end of the "stop."*

from last year's event, or use local horse trainers as judges. It can also be a lot of fun—a wonderful, low-stress entry point into showing horses. You may find kindred spirits—people just like you who want to spend their weekends showing horses. If you go to your local tack or feed store, you will find flyers advertising local horse shows hosted by such open clubs.

Breed Associations

If you are riding a horse that is registered with a breed association (like the American Quarter Horse Association, American Paint Horse Association, or Appaloosa Horse Club) you can compete in breed shows locally or at the national level. The breed association likely hosts a show that includes classes from many disciplines, just one of which will be reining. Some of the associations, the AQHA for example, have their own reining patterns with their own accredited judges and rulebooks. They may have also chosen to become affiliates of the NRHA and hold NRHA classes with NRHA-accredited judges.

NRHA Affiliate Clubs

There are over 100 associations worldwide that have chosen to pay an annual fee to be affiliated with the NRHA. As of 2009, 51 are based in the United States, 10 in Canada, and 26 in the rest of the world. These affiliate clubs hold shows with reining only and are responsible for reaching the grassroots reiners (you!) and offering a wide variety of classes to suit all skill levels.

Some classes will only require an affiliate club membership while others also require an NRHA membership. The affiliate may offer very beginner classes that do not require all the basic maneuvers, ideal for

1.5 The rollback requires the horse to turn almost 180 degrees on his haunches, and to go from a stop to a lope. It is a quick maneuver requiring more "muscle memory" than precise movements. Once horses learn it they can perform it very quickly.

green horse-and-rider combinations; they may adhere to the NRHA rulebook for certain classes (which are NRHA-approved) but have their own rules for entry-level classes (which are not NRHA-approved); or they may also participate in the NRHA Affiliate Championship Circuit that gives you the opportunity to compete against other affiliate club members from your region. Then in turn, the top riders from the region can compete in the Affiliate Championships for their continent like the North American Affiliate Championship.

FEI Competitions

Fédération Equestre Internationale (FEI) approved reining competition includes two major events: the World

NRHA Major Competitions

Because the NRHA is a large association, it hosts only two reining shows each year, but they are big. The NRHA Derby is for horses aged four, five, and six and is held every June, and the NRHA Futurity is for three-year-old horses and is held in November. Both take place in Oklahoma City, Oklahoma. At the NRHA Futurity the NRHA also hosts the North American Affiliate Championships. By competing in affiliate circuits across North America, competitors qualify to show at this event.

1.6 The back-up should be performed in a straight line with no resistance. This horse "gives" his nose and steps back willingly.

Rookie Days

The NRHA, recognizing the considerable grassroots growth in the reining industry has promoted an event called Rookie Days. What originally began in 2002 as an annual fundraiser for the Reining Horse Sports Foundation now occurs several times a year at locations all across the country.

At these events, well-known professional trainers come together to teach entry-level reiners the ins-and-outs of the sport. The format is set up like a reining clinic and beginning riders can receive one-on-one instruction. After the morning clinic sessions, mock competitions are held with clinic participants competing individually and in teams. Attending a Rookie Days, to either ride or watch, is a great opportunity to meet other beginners and make new friends interested in reining, like you.

Reining Masters (WRM) and the World Equestrian Games (WEG). Competitors for both are chosen by their countries (NAAs) through a series of qualifying events. The venue for the World Reining Masters alternates annually between a European and a North American location. The World Equestrian Games happen every four years and the location is chosen by the FEI after various countries submit their bids—much as the Olympic sites are chosen. For example, in 2002 WEG was held in Jerez, Spain, in 2006 in Aachen, Germany, and in 2010 in Lexington, Kentucky—the first time outside Europe.

THE ARENA

Reining arenas vary in size from small (60 by 100 feet) to large (200 by 400 feet) and anywhere in between. There is no standard size, although there are standard dimensions: arenas are rectangular in shape and have six markers placed inside the arena as reference points in the patterns. Markers are placed along the long sides of the wall or fence at the center point (on the wall) and at least 50 feet from each end wall.

Footing is of the utmost importance to reining horses. The ground in a reining arena is often meticulously groomed and care is taken to protect the base. The base is usually made of clay and it is packed and leveled before dirt and sand is placed on top of it. The depth of the sand can vary. The more dirt and sand, the harder your horse will have to push his hooves into the ground to slide because the deeper footing will provide more resistance.

The perfect depth can be hard to achieve. When the footing is too deep (too much sand) horses may get hurt when they try to stop and find it difficult. When the footing is too fast (too little sand), horses may get hurt when they go to stop and it is easy, causing their feet to slide far forward unexpectedly. Some horses may be better suited to either deep or fast ground, depending on what they are accustomed to and their stopping style.

Above all, the base should be smooth and without uneven patches that can cause a running or stopping horse to catch his foot and stumble. At fast speeds or during a maneuver such as a stop, tripping or catching a foot can be disastrous for horse and rider. The base should be redone every couple of years to ensure it is level, smooth, and safe.

WHAT HAPPENS AT A REINING SHOW?

When you attend your first reining show as a spectator, it may appear to be busier than a Los Angeles freeway. But once you get to know what is happening, it is much more orderly and structured than it first looks.

The closest show to where you live may be found through your local or regional NRHA Affiliate Association (see Appendix, p. 132) or online at www.nrha.com. It is important before you begin to compete in reining that you watch a reining show or two so that you have a better idea of what to expect. Learn more about showing in chapter 12, p. 85.

When you arrive, go to the registration desk or office. Depending on the size of the show, this might be a separate room or a table set to the side staffed by a volunteer who checks entries, assigns show numbers, and generally helps contestants figure out which end is up. Here you will be able to find the show bill or program that outlines the classes.

There will be a main competition arena and there might also be a separate riding warm-up area (or two, depending on the size of the show) where competitors and their horses get ready. Here you will see some horses at their worst and at their best. Some horses start out rambunctious and fresh but their riders want them focused and paying attention so they are loped in circles. Other riders may just climb on and warm up for a few minutes, perfecting a turn or stopping a few times.

Check the class schedule and look for the riders you may have noticed in the warm-up pen to see how their horses have calmed down (or not). When you see riders with a pale face, wide eyes, and holding their breath, you've likely found the beginner class. Here, it's not "deer in the headlights," it's "rookie in the show pen"!

Making mistakes is common in this class. If you have a copy of the pattern and are following along, you may notice several riders go off pattern. They may turn too many times, turn too few times, or their horse may not stop, or when he comes to a stop, he might not slide properly. This is all okay, because this is how beginners are expected to look.

Watch the open or professional classes. You'll notice that these riders have it more together. But even they may not be perfect. They will still go off pattern

The Fédération Equestre Internationale

The Fédération Equestre Internationale (FEI) is the association that governs the highest levels of competition in international and Olympic equestrian sports. There are currently only three Olympic equestrian sports (dressage, jumping, and eventing). Reining is the only Western riding sport approved by the FEI and is listed as a "non-Olympic sport" along with driving, endurance, vaulting, and the para-equestrian sports. The FEI is responsible for governing and overseeing the international (but non-Olympic) reining competitions (and their qualifiers) such as the World Reining Masters and the World Equestrian Games. Qualifying shows are often referred to as Concours de Reining International (or CRI) competitions and may be held in conjunction with NRHA-sanctioned events. A CRI-A has prize money of over $10,000 and a CRI-B less than $10,000. These shows use NRHA patterns and judges. Note: The International Affiliate Program (IAP) of the NRHA is not associated with the FEI.

and over- or under-spin. This is normal. Reining is a pressure-intensive sport and even the best have made critical mistakes during a run.

Longtime trainer and NRHA judge Mario Boisjoli, from Agua Dulce in California, encourages his rookies to watch the open riders so they can see how a run is supposed to go. "I do believe that people learn a lot by watching, and they kind of soak it in, and see what it's supposed to look like. If I wanted to learn how to play the violin I wouldn't listen to an eight-year-old scratch away," says Boisjoli, "but if I heard a real violinist I would say, 'Oh, well *that's* how it's supposed to sound.'"

Scoring

As soon as the competing horse and rider enter the reining arena, they are given a baseline score of "70," which denotes an average run and—depending on the quality of performance of the maneuvers we covered earlier—their score may increase or decrease from there. The individual maneuvers are scored in ½-point increments from a low of minus-1½ (very poor) to a high of +1½ (excellent). The total of these scores is combined with the baseline of 70 and any penalties are deducted to calculate the rider's final score. For a complete outline of how scoring works, see chapter 8, p. 53.

Volunteering

Putting on horse shows is a lot of work, often performed solely by volunteers. Almost any association will be happy and grateful for a couple of extra hands and volunteering is a great way to learn about reining. You get to see it from ground level, right in the dust, standing next to trainers and coaches who are helping prepare their riders. There is always a need for someone to run the in-gate, take entries, scribe, or help with set-up and take-down.

By volunteering, you get to meet other local competitors as well as their trainers. You'll find that there is a lot of advice passed between riders and trainers on the ground: discussions on which bits they like and why; bloodlines they prefer; coaching tips. Just "hanging around" in the dirt near the warm-up pen or in-gate can be a great education.

To find out how to volunteer, contact the show manager or NRHA representative listed in the show program.

Scribing

By far the best way to get to know what is expected in reining competition is to volunteer as a scribe—other than the judge, he has the best seat in the house (see photo 8.3, p. 58). You may have noticed there is always one sitting next to the judge, holding a clipboard, and periodically writing comments since the judge cannot chance missing part of the run to look down.

The scribe records maneuver scores and penalties as well as tallying the total score and calling it into the announcer or show office. You only need a basic understanding of penalties and some reasonable math skills to be able to do this job and the process is actually quite easy and very educational.

You get to see the run from inside the arena, hear each maneuver score and penalty as it happens, and may be able to ask the judge a question between horses to gain insight into why a horse marked plus or minus on his maneuver, where the particular penalty occurred, or what the rider could have done to improve his score.

HOW MUCH WILL SHOWING COST?

Let's face it. Horse sports are not cheap. And showing makes them that much more expensive. In addition to the outside regular horse maintenance expenses we are all aware of—board, farrier, healthcare—there are specific reining show-related expenses, too.

The Horse

This is the largest expense. At the time of writing, you can expect to pay a minimum of $10,000 for a trained reining horse, more if you're looking for a very well trained one. However, as with everything, you can find horses that cost far less and far more! A reining horse's value is determined by his age—too old, he has fewer sound years left, too young, he isn't experienced enough; his amount of training in the sport of reining; his health and soundness history; and the amount of money he has won (the NRHA tracks every penny a horse wins in NRHA-approved classes). Read more about what is required of a reining horse in chapter 12, p. 85.

Transportation

If you want your own truck and trailer, you will have related expenses: for example, a $30,000 truck and a $20,000 horse trailer plus fuel costs. Or, if you purchase a trailer with living quarters (a "camperized" compartment at its front end), its cost can be easily $50,000 or more. Another option is to have your trainer haul your horse to a show. He will likely charge you a fee per mile. Or, travel with a friend or someone who owns their equipment and split the fuel costs.

Horse Shoes

Specialized sliding plates are necessary and they need to be replaced or reset about every six weeks, depending on rate of wear and hoof growth. Shoeing expenses vary by region, but count on an average $100 to $200 for a new set of shoes, less for a reset.

Memberships

Most clubs and associations require you to join if you

plan to compete at their shows. An annual regional club membership may be $30 to $50, whereas an NRHA membership in 2009 is $95 for a General (unrestricted, cannot compete in Non Pro classes) or Non Pro membership, and $35 for Youths. You do not have to purchase a membership until you are ready to compete.

As some shows are hosted by multiple associations, you may require more than one membership, but do not purchase more memberships than you need; most can be purchased at the time of a show, and on the showgrounds, so you can confirm with the show secretary which memberships are required. For example, you may enter a class that is approved by the hosting affiliate, a breed association, and the NRHA—a total of three memberships. Or, you may attend a show that has NRHA-approved classes, but if you are not competing in one of those classes, you do not require an NRHA membership.

Show Expenses

Each class you enter has an entry fee, which is typically 10 percent of the prize money available, so if there is $2,000 to be won, your fee is $200. At smaller shows, entering can cost as little as $10 for a "jackpot" class in which all fees are pooled together with the winner taking a large percentage, and second- and third-place riders receiving incrementally smaller portions.

Every show also has individual expenses such as stall fees (for overnight stabling), ground fees (for horses not staying overnight), judges fees (your contribution toward paying the judges), and (possibly) extra charges for bedding or hay when you need to purchase it at the show.

"Living Quarters" Trailers

A "living-quarters" trailer is normally an "angle-haul" trailer (a trailer that allows horses to stand on a slant inside) with a compartment at the front that has been customized for sleeping and other comforts of home. These can be as sparse as a simple bed, mirror, and no insulation, or they can be luxurious: basics might include a bed, kitchenette, closet space for your clothes, and even a toilet and shower. Some of these trailers cost hundreds of thousands of dollars.

Money-Saving Ideas for the Competitor on a Budget

Share overnight expenses with a friend (split costs of a hotel, camper, or a trailer with living quarters).

If someone has a trailer with living quarters that they are not using, offer to feed her horses in the morning in exchange for allowing you to stay there.

When hauling to the show, split fuel costs with someone else.

Conserve fuel by keeping your truck's engine well maintained and tire pressure at the correct levels. Check for a local mechanic who specializes in engine modifications that could help you with vehicle performance.

Take your own bedding and hay to avoid paying premium prices at the showgrounds.

Buy a longer term or lifetime membership in the organizations of your choice—it results in greater savings over the span of your show career.

2 Which Comes First: The Horse or the Trainer?

Reining has caught your eye: the skilled horse-manship, the union of horse and rider, and the spirit of competition. Whatever it is, you want to be in on it.

When embarking on a reining "career," I believe the trainer comes before the horse because it is important to seek input from professionals: If you start to rein or begin to compete on your own, you may make costly mistakes. As you may know (and it's the same with horses *and* people), when you learn the wrong way first, you will have a hard time *un*learning and then *re*learning. It's much better to start off on the right foot and get it right the first time.

DO *YOU* NEED A TRAINER?

When attending a show, you'll notice that a reiner often has a bunch of helpers around him, brushing his horse's tail, straightening and dusting his chaps, or trying to calm his nerves. Usually included in this group is the rider's trainer.

Many reining trainers can *train* both horse and rider, but not all can *coach* effectively in competition, so it is important that the trainer you choose has coaching skills to help *you* succeed, not just your horse. Just as a football player looks to his coach for inspira-

tion, guidance, training advice, and correction, a rookie reiner needs a trainer with the talent and ability to coach him in the same ways. It is not enough to just train the horse and then stick the rider on top and say, "Ok, now follow the pattern." Reining is much more complicated than that.

A good trainer will help you understand the psychology of showing, take the time to understand your unique needs, and coach you successfully.

You do not necessarily need a trainer to compete in reining. There are books and videos on how to train your horse to perform the necessary maneuvers. However, a good trainer knows you and your horse and can be the number-one person on your "team" (that group of "helpers" I mentioned earlier). He will be waiting at the gate to tell you just what you've done wrong and where you need to improve. A video cannot tell you, "You forgot to keep your hand in the middle of your horse again," or "Don't think about that last run, here's what we are going to focus on this time."

If you do not have access to a trainer, you need to have consistency in your self-directed training. Whether you are faithfully following one program by video or a series of clinics, or you are "hauling in" and taking lessons from a local trainer but not regularly riding with him, uniformity is key.

HOW TO FIND A TRAINER

In the previous chapter, I described the types of shows you can attend and where they may be held. At these shows you will likely find various trainers' information pinned on bulletin boards or listed in the show program. You can also watch the professionals riding in the warm-up and show pens for an idea of their riding style. Make a note of their names and locations as they could be in your area and taking on students. Wander through the barns and stall areas because there may be business cards on tables set up at each trainer's stabling area.

Talk to some of the competitors to find out who they ride with, and who they recommend—and don't just ask the winning riders! Keep an open mind when you talk to a trainer's clients. Whether speaking to a disgruntled former customer or an elated current one, you are unlikely to get an unbiased opinion. But you can get a good idea of training rates, lesson schedules, and the number of other beginners in a barn.

Watch a particular trainer's clients showing and observe them interacting in the warm-up pen. "If you like the way they ride their horses and how they talk to their clients, that's a good sign," says Mario Boisjoli. "Some trainers are more tactful than others, and even the ones that aren't tactful may still get good results with people who need that kind of pressure. But maybe for some people that wouldn't suit, you need to know a little bit about yourself."

You need to consider that one type of training will not work for everyone. What do you know about yourself? Did you compete in track and field or swimming or basketball when young? Are you competitive? Are you a Type-A personality or are you laid back and mellow? Do you want to be pushed or do you want to do things in your own time? Knowing the answers to these questions will help you to find the trainer that suits you best.

Trainers that are looking for students also advertise in horse periodicals, at tack stores, or on Web sites. Make a list of the ones in your area. Some trainers choose to take on only experienced riders, others focus on beginners, and some do both.

"The best way to get consistency is to pick a trainer or program and let that trainer or program have a chance to work," says Boisjoli. "Maybe at some point you say,

2.1 *A trainer can greatly help you navigate your show career.*

'I need a new trainer or program,' but once you select it, give it a chance to work before you move on."

Boisjoli cautions beginning riders from picking and choosing from a smorgasbord of clinicians. "I don't want to tell people they can't go or shouldn't go to clinics, but a lot of people run around doing what I call 'taking a poll.' If you are riding in one program and then you go to the Andrea Fappani (a Futurity and Derby champion) clinic and you try to pluck out, 'Well, Andrea holds the reins this way when he spins,' or 'Andrea Fappani does this with his legs when he spins...' it may not necessarily dovetail into everything else you're already doing."

QUESTIONS TO ASK A PROSPECTIVE TRAINER

Once you have determined your "short list," call to request a meeting and watch him teach a lesson. Have a list of questions prepared:

What are your barn hours?
How much do lessons cost?
Are the lessons private or in groups?

2.2 *Interaction between a trainer and student can be personalized to fit that particular relationship. It should be based on trust and open communication.*

How much is boarding?

Which shows do you attend?

Do all your students show?

Do you teach clinics regularly?

Who are your most successful students?

Do you have horses for sale?

Do you have lesson horses?

Will you help me buy a horse or evaluate mine?

Is your barn busy at certain times?

There are training facilities that only take boarders who keep and ride their horse there. Some offer lessons to people who keep their horse elsewhere, while others will also take a horse in for training.

While you are visiting, ask current students about the barn and what to expect. You should determine the schedule you are looking for—do you prefer evening or weekend lessons?—to be sure it doesn't conflict with the barn's schedule. For example, when a facility has many disciplines being trained there or has a large number of boarders that don't ride reiners, there may

be nights when the arena is open to one type of riding only. Or, there may be weekend afternoons that have events scheduled like regular clinics or lessons.

If you keep your horse at another facility (or maybe your home) and haul in for lessons, there may be a special schedule for "haul-in" lessons so that the riders at the facility know when to expect a busy barn. Some barns (and trainers) have no set schedule at all, maybe only barn hours (lights out at 9:00 P.M. for instance).

All trainers have a particular style or way of teaching that works well for them, but the great trainers change their style just enough to fit each student. Therefore, it's important to view lessons in progress so you can observe how the trainer interacts with riders. Some trainers speak softly and have a preference for getting on your horse and showing you what to do; others speak louder and stand for the entire lesson. And, there are trainers who give a lot of feedback while others offer very little. (You may want to review "trainer speak" on p. 114 where I provide a translation of all the "catch phrases" you are likely to hear a trainer say. These can be hard to understand, at first!)

As I mentioned, good trainers like Roberta McCarty, who has coached many riders to the NRHA Rookie of the Year finals, change their teaching style with each rider. "You can't teach a 14-year-old teenager the same that you would teach a 60-year-old business executive," says McCarty who finds that the younger the student, the less she questions a trainer's directives.

"If you tell a 14-year-old to go run her horse down to a stop, she'll do it, no questions asked. Whereas the business executive is going to look at you like, 'Are you nuts? Why would I want to do that?' Kids don't ask why. They are used to taking orders and if they like you—as a rule, if you are training them, they like and respect you—then when you tell them to go do something, even if it's difficult or a little outrageous, they say, 'Okay!'"

McCarty doesn't take herself too seriously and cautions riders from taking lessons from a trainer who seems to be on a "power trip." Such a trainer can be identified by his behavior: not fully explaining the reason behind requests when asked; expecting total compliance without question; and treating the rider without respect or assuming that the rider cannot learn the technique but only follow direction. A trainer should be willing to answer questions about the theory behind the practical application of training techniques and not leave you in the dark.

"I never really tell people to do something just because I said so: I always give them a reason," says McCarty. "If we are loping and doing a guiding exercise and I tell them to turn right, then we'll talk about why I'm telling them to do that. It's not because I've arbitrarily decided to give them orders."

She also asks her students a lot of questions. By their answers, she can tell if they understand her instructions. The relationship between a trainer and a rider is that of a teacher and a student—to help teach *why* things are done, not just when and how.

STARTING OFF ON THE RIGHT FOOT

The trainer-client relationship should be mutually beneficial. While money will change hands as you pay for a service, this is not an impersonal business transaction. Both parties should expect open, honest communication and a deepening trust and respect for each other as the relationship develops. It is crucial that you start off on the right foot. Clear, open, and honest communication is the key to any successful relationship. Despite our best intentions, we tend to get emotional when it comes to our horses. Add in the stress and strain of competition and the financial commitments, and any unaddressed frustrations will compound over time.

When it comes to setting up a client-trainer agreement, there is no "one way" to do it. There are too many variables: for example, you might want to ride your own horse, need to use a lesson horse, or be in the market to buy a new one. And, instead of keeping your horse with the trainer, you might want to keep him at home, or board at a different facility and just haul in for lessons. You must decide what is important to you.

To facilitate communication, clearly outline your expectations. For example:

▶ I will receive a minimum of X lesson(s) every week.

▶ The trainer will inform me with at least 24 hours notice of any change of lesson time.

▶ My horse will be ridden at least X times per week (when in training).

▶ We will develop a plan by spring for showing during the coming year.

▶ We will choose an appropriate horse for my abilities and the trainer will tell me when he feels I am ready to move up to a different horse.

▶ We discuss all fees above and beyond regular training or coaching fees.

Do not be surprised if your trainer has certain expectations of you. For example:

▶ His professional opinion will carry weight when making horse-purchasing decisions.

▶ You will show up on time for lessons or give proper notice.

▶ You will support and encourage your barnmates at all shows (those people who ride at the same barn and "stall" together at shows).

▶ You will commit to the training and showing goals outlined at the beginning of the year.

Being upfront about your ability to make financial and time commitments is important early on, especially once you begin to set goals with your trainer. Winning a regional year end award will not require the same financial commitment as showing at the NRHA Futurity in Oklahoma City—the pinnacle show of the industry. (In chapter 13, p. 93, I've included a section called Planning and Goal-Setting that expands upon this idea. In addition, I address the issue of transitioning to a new trainer and upgrading your mount in chapter 16, p. 113).

Safety First

When competing, child reiners may be required to wear a helmet rather than a Western hat (see p. 44 for more information on attire). The NRHA does not require this; however, local clubs may have rules that supersede NRHA regulations.

2.4 *A quiet, well mannered reining horse, like this one, can provide a great confidence boost to a young child who is just learning the ropes.*

2.3 *Children are more than capable of riding reining patterns with the help of the right horse.*

WHEN THE TRAINER ISN'T FOR YOU: YOUTH REINING

If you are reading this book to learn more about getting your child started in reining, that is wonderful news. The sport of reining is very "child-friendly" and there are some great places to start. The NRHA has even developed a pattern expressly for reiners age 10 and under called the "Short Stirrup" pattern. This eliminates the flying lead change, making it a manageable class for children as young as six. After they have mastered this class, they can move up to NRHA-approved youth reining classes. In addition, many NRHA affiliates, 4-H groups, and small regional horse show clubs offer non-NRHA-approved, introductory level reining classes for children. I provide more information on youth reining in chapter 9 (p. 59).

Buying a reining horse for your child is a major undertaking. He must be quiet, have an amicable disposition, and be considered "bombproof." Unfortunately, the more broke the horse, the more expensive he becomes. Expect to pay more money for one that can perform all the maneuvers (I tell you more about this type of horse in chapter 4, p. 22). Again, finding the right trainer, first, can help you and your child get started on the right foot. Trainers often have leads on well-broke horses that are about to be outgrown or will soon be for sale, and they can help you weigh the pros and cons of "imperfect" mounts if you're searching on a budget.

Choosing a trainer for your child can be nerve-wracking. Any parent knows that a coach or teacher can have a profound affect on a child in many ways so it pays to look for a trainer that has an outlook that matches your child's. Luckily, some trainers specialize in young riders and have the attitude and patience to teach kids at all skill levels.

3 Your Reining Partner— The Horse

Just about any horse can learn the basics of reining. Even mules have been taught to rein (though they are not allowed to show in NRHA classes). The variable is how *well* he can learn to do it. If your goal is to become competitive then you should purchase a horse with the body type and mind to perform the maneuvers. This chapter will discuss those two ideals: the physical and the mental attributes of a reining horse.

One breed of horse dominates the reining pen. The American Quarter Horse has both the mechanical structure and the attitude especially well-suited for learning and performing the reining moves. Granted, there are many different body types to be found in the breed, but overall, Quarter Horses have common characteristics that I will discuss in detail in this chapter.

Other breeds such as American Paint Horses, Appaloosas, Morgans, and Arabians have also had significant success in the show pen.

THE IDEAL BODY TYPE

Regardless of the breed, there are characteristics that indicate a horse might make a good reiner. NRHA Hall of Famer Bob Loomis is known as one of the industry's top breeders. His treatise on the correct build of a reining horse in his book *Reining: The Art of Perfor-*
mance in Horses* (EquiMedia, 1990) simply cannot be improved upon.

Neck and Topline "The neck should be moderately long and clean...it should come straight out of the body with a slight elevation from the withers. Medium length is best. A horse with a short neck has a tendency to move his shoulders too quickly. A horse with a long neck has a tendency to be a little too loose and it is difficult to keep his spine aligned or straight in the maneuvers...the ideal neck should be the same length as the horse's shoulder, back and hip."

Take a measuring tape and see if your horse measures up: the poll to withers measurement should be the same as the withers to croup; the croup to point of the hip should measure the same as the withers to point of the shoulder.

Shoulders and Withers "The length of a horse's stride is determined by his shoulder angle. Sloping or well-angled shoulders permit a horse to reach a good distance over the ground...a horse with long, sloping shoulders and high withers usually has a large heart girth. The bigger the heart girth, the larger the lung capacity. The more air a horse can take in, the more endurance he has and the sounder he stays."

Back and Loins "Truly athletic horses have strong backs and loins and know how to use them when they

3.1 A–D   *Many different breeds compete in reining, but the American Quarter Horse (A) dominates. The Appaloosa (B), American Paint Horse (C), and the Arabian (D) are also strongly represented. Some examples of successful competitors from each breed: (A) Quarter Horse: Who Whiz It, (B) Appaloosa: MA Thunderstorm, (C) Paint Horse: Spooks Gotta Gun, (D) Arabian: Zallas Classic Zee.*

perform. Watch a horse that can stop deep and hard. He doesn't lock his hocks and skid. He drops his loins underneath himself. It is effortless for a horse with a short back, strong loin, long hip, and short cannon bone to stop."

Hips   "Hips should be long and powerful with hocks set low to the ground in a straight line down from the hip. Power in a horse comes from his hindquarters."

Legs   "Forearms should be long for plenty of length and sweep in the stride...Pasterns should be the same angle as the shoulders. Both are the horse's shock absorption mechanism...Cannon bones should be in proportion to the horse's size and short compared to the forearm...short cannon bones are strong and increase a horse's stability."

Feet   "Good, hard, well-shaped feet are essential to any performance horse...large feet are not ugly. They serve as excellent weight-bearing surfaces for a 1,000-pound animal. In addition to sufficient size, good feet are oval-shaped and have tough horn, large heels, healthy frogs, hard soles, and well-developed bars of the heels."

Heart "We often hear that a horse with a lot of guts has a big heart. While we can never actually see the size of the heart, there is physical evidence for the saying. A horse with a big heart pumps more blood. Blood and oxygen give a horse strength. Therefore, a horse with a large heart has more stamina."

Don Burt has been a proponent of the stalwart Quarter Horse body and its ability to perform reining. And Burt should know. In 2003 he was given the Pfizer Animal Health and American Horse Publications Equine Industry Vision Award for his dedication to the breed, which he's been involved with since the 1930s.

In his book, Loomis outlined his friend Don Burt's thoughts about what a reining horse should look like and the "trapezoid body type" that he theorized was ideal. During a speech at a seminar that Loomis had attended, Burt had revealed his test for correct conformation in the reining horse:

Step One: Look at the body only. Divide it into thirds. The first third is from the point of the shoulder to the girth line, which is the line drawn between the back of the withers down under the chest behind the foreleg. The middle third is from the girth line to a line drawn from the top of the croup down the flank. The rear third is from the last line described to the point of the buttocks. The horse should divide equally (fig. 3.2 A).

Step Two: While observing the body, draw an imaginary line starting at the point of the shoulder. Make a straight line to the point of the buttocks. From there draw a line to the top of the croup. From the top of the croup, draw a line to the withers, and from the withers draw a line to the point of the shoulder. This figure is a trapezoid (fig. 3.2 B).

The front sloping line from the point of the shoulders to the withers is an indication of the horse's speed and endurance. At the correct angle (as outlined in the trapezoid) the horse

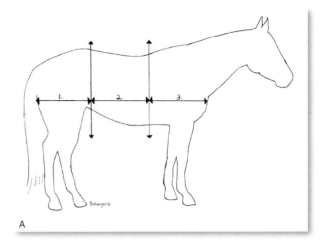

A

B

3.2 A & B   *By dividing your horse's body into thirds, you can get a good idea of his conformation (A). The trapezoid body type has long been regarded as ideal (B).*

has enough speed and endurance to succeed as a reining horse. If the angle is too shallow the endurance will suffer, too steep and he will not be fast enough. The line from the point of the buttocks to the top of the croup is an indication of the horse's power. Again, too shallow and there will not be enough power for a reining horse. The line from the top of the croup to the withers is an indication of topline strength: if a topline is not strong enough, the horse will not have the consistent ability to stop properly, which requires lifting his shoulders and rounding his back.

The key to this trapezoid and the usefulness of the horse is the bottom line, the longer the better. A horse that is divided evenly into thirds will have a short topline and a long bottom line. The matching angles are all important for balance. Angles that are equal are better than angles that are mismatched. Most horses are unbalanced. Those that have correct balance happen to be the champions. Angles are the key to performance.

Ode to the Cannon Bone

The cannon bones of a reining horse endure a lot of stress. Running hard to a stop is stressful on all four legs and spinning involves the front legs crossing over one another repeatedly and with speed. This is why reining horses wear leg gear such as polo wraps and splint boots (discussed on p. 40) to protect them from concussive injury and strains to the tendons and ligaments found at the back of the cannon bone. When this bone is too long, it loses the strength and stability it needs to carry the rest of the horse's body through athletic movements.

Bob Loomis, on a horse's heart:

"A horse with a big heart is worthless if he never gives it to you. That's what separates the great horses from the average ones. A horse's heart has a lot to do with his mental attitude. It has to do with how much he lets you use him, how much of himself he gives to you."

On a good reining horse:

"The magical combination in a good reining horse is one that is light and responsive when you handle it, yet extremely quiet with a calm, cool-headed personality."

On the horse's mind:

"Trainability is the willingness to accept training, a desire to obey."

THE IDEAL MIND

Regardless of breed, there is one characteristic that every reining horse must possess to be successful: a good mind. So, what makes a "good-minded" horse? When you review the *NRHA Handbook*, you find the answer. You may recall Jim Willoughby's paragraph that I included in chapter 1 (see p. 1). There he expresses, "To rein a horse is not only to guide him, but also to control his every movement. The best reined horse should be willingly guided or controlled with little or no apparent resistance and dictated to completely. Any movement on his own must be considered a lack of control."

The mind of a reining horse should be trainable. Without this very important attribute, you can have a horse with ideal conformation and athleticism, but he will not be worth the hay you feed him because you will not be able to train him successfully to use his natural ability.

Your horse must allow you to guide and control his movements without resistance while displaying a good attitude and confidence. There are many different mental attitudes. Which kind of horse do you own or are you considering buying? Let's look at four archetypes:

Type A Aggressive   This horse is the first to be fed in the morning because he paws in his stall if you aren't quick enough—he's been waiting all night, after all. When you get on his back to ride, he walks off before you've even swung your leg all the way over the saddle. But he enjoys being good at his job and displays confidence in maneuvers when he has mastered them. He never has to be asked twice to go faster and has powerful stops. To ride this horse, you sometimes need to get out of his way and let him do his job.

Type B Socializer   He's the horse calling to his buddies from the outdoor arena because he just cannot bear to be alone. He has a hard time focusing on you when you are riding in a warm-up because, to him, a strange horse is just a horse he hasn't met yet. He is well-meaning but tends to get distracted easily. However, when he has a job to do, it's fun to ride him because he has a desire to please. He puts extra effort into fixing mistakes when you've corrected him and he finally "gets" what he's supposed to do. To ride this horse, give him a lot of positive reinforcement in the form of pats and praise after a job well done.

Type C Detail Organizer This horse doesn't like change in his routine. He knows when it's time to come in from his paddock and is frustrated when you are late. He likes to warm up the same way every day. On the positive side, he's a workhorse that values studious labor and lots of it. To be a success with him, don't give him too much time off his regular routine.

Type D Dependable This mellow and amicable horse does not require a lot of correcting, but when you do he accepts it and tries not to make the same mistake. He walks to you to be haltered and brought in from the field, or stands quietly in his stall waiting to be fed. This horse will not only be successful with you, but will go on to help other beginners in their first reining shows. Just keep him healthy and fit and don't expect him to perform too hard for too long.

The ideal reining horse has some of each of the qualities I've just outlined. You want a horse to aggressively perform the maneuvers, to desire to be rewarded for his efforts, to enjoy the job for the job's sake, and to accept training and correction with a positive attitude. But keep in mind that horses do have personality types, and it isn't fair to expect your Type B horse to behave like a Type D horse overnight. Accept that you can train behaviors, but not traits that are innate to the horse's personality type.

Learning to work with the type of horse that you have is very important. There is an oft-repeated phrase in reining: "Show the horse that you have." This means that you need to train and ride your horse, not the horse that you wish he'd become. Keep in mind his individuality, capitalize on his strengths, and manage his weaknesses.

4 Finding the Right Reining Horse

Roberta McCarty, whom I introduced in chapter 2, has helped most of her beginners find the perfect show horse for their first reining years. She starts out by watching them ride on a horse she knows well and is broke to her program. This helps her determine if the rider is aggressive or timid, and whether he needs a lazy horse or can handle one that needs a skilled rider.

A major challenge McCarty often faces is the rider who already has a horse. "A lot of times rookies come to us with a horse they have raised themselves or just fallen in love with, and it's not suitable for the goals we've discussed. People end up with a horse and then set goals for themselves instead of doing it the other way around. In a perfect world, I'd like someone to come to me and say, 'I want a horse that will make me competitive in the rookie-level classes and these are my goals.'"

As a rider with an eye to successful performance, you need to be realistic, says McCarty. Everyone wants to fall in love with his horse and most think their horse is one of a kind. But there are many horses out there and many different partnerships to be made. "I tend to be very upfront with people about their horses and not 'babysit' them through bad horses because ultimately the goals are not going to be reached, which is very frustrating. I've had it happen where people have had a horse that is not suitable for what they want to do. They stick with and put money into the horse, and they basically 'burn out' of the show horse business."

You can easily become disenchanted with the entire system of putting money into a seemingly bottomless pit of horse show entry fees, while seeing little or no return because you are not on a horse that is going to help you be successful.

Recently McCarty helped a new client purchase a nine-year-old gelding. After discussing goals and determining the rider's skills, she set out to find the ideal horse. "He's an absolute saint. He's never going to go mark a score of 72 and that's fine. He's fine for the lady, he's safe for her, he does what she tells him to do, and that's the kind of horse you are looking for." Eventually, this client's ability will outgrow her horse's ability and both of them will move on—the horse to a new partnership and a new beginner to take care of, and the rider to a new horse with more potential.

SPECIAL NEEDS FOR THE NOVICE REINER

What sets apart a good horse for the rookie rider from the more high-performance athletes in reining is his *mind*. He needs to be honest enough to both build the rider's confidence at home and take care of him in the show pen.

Cory Hutchings, a successful trainer from Arlington, Washington, has specific criteria he looks for when shopping for a horse for a first-time reiner. He wants something that is "honest," which to him means the horse doesn't change personality or temperament between home and show. A horse may display some behavioral changes, but overall, he must be the same horse that you loaded on the trailer when you left the barn. Hutchings also likes to buy a horse has been shown enough and consistently so that he can have a fairly good idea of what kind of horse to expect in the show pen. He looks for one that allows the beginning rider to show at his own pace, and focus on doing maneuvers correctly, so the horse must be able and willing to move slowly and correctly.

Hutchings weeds out horses with a commonly seen undesirable trait of being "ring sour." These will often "cheat" on their riders in the pen and not perform to the best of their ability. This trait shows up most frequently in the rundown to the stop. A horse is supposed to wait for the rider to tell him when to speed up, but a "show smart" horse will simply speed up when he is pointed in a straight line in the pattern.

Before making a recommendation, Hutchings watches the horse being put through different maneuvers and also rides him to test his level of competency.

Because there are more stops in a pattern than any other maneuver, this tends to be a focus of many buyers. The "stop" is the key. "You want to be able to learn to stop on a horse that does it well," says Hutchings. "I want one to perform a sliding stop even if you are falling off." This is especially important because it can be easy for riders to be hurt or scared by a horse that stops improperly by bracing with the front legs or not rounding his back during the stop. Just one improperly executed bone-jarring stop that throws you into the front of your saddle can be enough to change the way your body anticipates a stop. When you stiffen, thinking that it's going to hurt, you get in the way of your horse's ability to stop.

MAKE A PLAN BEFORE BUYING

To ensure that you purchase the best horse for your needs, make a plan:

"Big Stops"

Some reining horses have the ability to perform exceptionally well in a stop. A horse with a "big stop" pushes very hard into the ground with his hind legs during the stop, slides for a long way, and maintains his balance easily with his front legs. This big stop is very easy to ride because it is smooth and does not jar the rider. There is no other way to stop in reining. I discuss the mechanics of this on p. 68.

Working for Commission

Commissions are common in the horse industry. The buyer generally pays a commission to the person who helped him find the horse, and the seller pays a commission to the person who helped him sell horse. Normally the buyer and seller have their respective trainers complete the sale. The most common commission is 10 percent but can be negotiated.

1   Decide your objectives and goals. These can be short- or long-term and include specific accomplishments like placing in the "Top 10" in your region, or future plans like eventually passing on a gelding to family members or breeding a mare.

2   Know what you will not accept. You may rule out a stallion because of stabling concerns or horses with conformation issues that could prevent, for example, a good "stop."

3   Know your personal drawbacks. For example, if changing leads is a challenge, try to find a horse that is very good at this maneuver.

4   Shop with accountability. This is why shopping with a trainer is a good idea. He can dissuade you from buying a horse when you are overlooking his flaws because he is "really cute." If you don't have a trainer, make a list of what you need and don't deviate from it.

5   Test rides are mandatory. It is crucial that someone trustworthy (like your trainer or a more experienced rider) rides the horse before you buy him.

Reviewing Sale Videos

When a prospect is located far away, the seller will often have a video available, either online or in some format he can send you. When watching video, note the overall appearance of the horse: Is he a nice mover? Does he have a nice profile? Does he look happy to be doing his job? However, remember that the video should only tell you whether or not you want to know more about the horse; it should not make the purchasing decision for you.

Signs of a Ring Sour Horse

Pins ears when asked for maneuvers

Is unwilling to enter the show pen

Gives a lot of attention to the out-gate

Kicks, bucks, or exhibits bad behavior in the show pen

Has a poor attitude in the stall at showgrounds

Won't load easily into a trailer

And you don't want this person just to lope the horse around and get off—he needs to *really* ride him: test every maneuver; correct the horse to see how he accepts it; ride with and without spurs; see what he does when the reins are loose or taut. The point is to test the prospective horse's reaction to a different rider.

6 Have a "vet check" or "pre-purchase exam" done by your veterinarian. If your veterinarian is not located close enough to the horse to go for a farm visit, have him recommend a vet in the appropriate area. Your vet can also have X-rays sent to him for review. Often you can put a deposit down on a horse pending the pre-purchase exam.

THE OLDER, EXPERIENCED HORSE

It can be a good idea to buy an older, experienced horse when you start reining: one that has seen the inside of a show pen many times before and won't get flustered when you are nervous and forget how to cue him or neglect to breathe through the entire pattern!

Mario Boisjoli, whom you first met in chapter 1, believes that buying an older horse is a great way for a rookie to get started, especially if finances are a concern. "Even if the horse has been shown a lot, we school him past issues like being ring sour (see sidebar) because he can still do his job well. You can get a lot of mileage out of a good older horse."

When shopping for the older horse, make sure that his having shown or "won" are not your only criteria. A horse that has been "over-shown" may be ring sour and bring his bad attitude into the pen. The ideal older reining horse has a balance of show pen experience combined with a good attitude about his job and the solid training to do it.

Health Issues

There are specific details to check into with an older horse, especially one that has been a performance horse and that you expect to continue to perform well in the future.

Common lameness may occur in the hock, stifle, or back, most often caused by arthritis or degenerative joint disease. An older horse whose conformation is not correct (see p. 17) will be more prone to the detrimental long-term effects of performance. As any engineer will tell you, a poorly constructed frame will experience more wear and tear at the stress points (joints) than one that is perfectly constructed to withstand stress. (This is true for a horse of any age, but purchasing an older horse means that the evidence of this stress may now begin to manifest in the form of lameness.) In addition, synovial fluid, the lubricant in your horse's joints, is constantly replacing itself until about the horse's fifteenth year when the fluid begins to lose its viscosity. This can cause joint friction and consequent inflammation.

So, before buying the older animal, discuss this horse's condition with your veterinarian during the pre-purchase exam. He may prescribe treatment and maintenance plans that include scheduled rest, anti-inflammatory medication or supplements; suggest you keep an eye out for swelling or heat in the horse's joints; and possibly order annual X-rays. If you are interested in homeopathic or naturopathic treatments you can seek out a veterinarian through the American Veterinary Naturopathic Association (www.avna. us). You can also speak with other professionals such as equine chiropractors, herbalists, and massage therapists. Ensure that whichever treatment you undertake, you do so under the advisement of an accredited professional and you keep your veterinarian informed.

As mentioned the benefits an older horse can bring (stability, dependability, experience, and safety) can far outweigh any concessions you may need to make because of his age.

THE YOUNG HORSE

Reining horses are commonly started under saddle at age two. They are showing by the time they are three. Horses under the age of three are often offered for considerably less money because they have not yet proven that they can compete. The lower price tag can be tempting; but it comes with a word or two of warning.

Riding and training a younger horse is a challenge. A younger horse will not be as steady as an older one and will have plenty of growing to do—both physical and mental—before he can be considered a good prospect for a novice reiner, even if you have ridden in other disciplines. Because he hasn't been shown a lot, you won't know what he's like in the show pen until he throws a curve ball at you, like suddenly missing his lead changes or getting fractious in his rundowns. What makes a young horse an even harder puzzle to figure out is that he might try new ways to trick you. It may seem like a process of elimination as he tries something different in each class.

If you are easily flustered and have never ridden a young horse before, it can be scary to feel a loss of control when a horse acts up. But, youngsters act up. Just like children, they often have to test boundaries to determine what is acceptable.

The Ideal Age

If you are set on a younger horse, the youngest you should consider when starting out is a five-year-old. By then, a horse has matured mentally and physically. He's probably had enough riding so that he can be considered broke. Keep in mind that some breeds (Arabians, for example) mature later.

Mario Boisjoli, on not "skimping" on the horse:

"Get the best horse you can afford. Everything else: board, training, shoeing, show entries, stalls, trucks and trailers ... can be bought for less or you can make do with less. You don't have to hire a trainer; you can take lessons when you need it. Just don't skimp on the horse. Forgo the new horse trailer or something if you have to. I have seen people that have the nicest truck and the nicest trailer, but a cheap horse. They arrive and look great, but then they get on the horse and look terrible."

5 Care of the Competitive Reining Horse

THE HORSE AS AN ATHLETE

There are several things that an athlete needs to be a success: adequate training, mental preparation, proper nourishment, and appropriate health care. Your job is to provide your reining horse all of these.

Adequate Training

▶ Build up muscles and endurance by spending enough time exercising and practicing prior to showing.

▶ Provide proper warm ups at shows.

▶ Train individual maneuvers to ensure they are performed properly and without error.

Mental Preparation

▶ Take care not to over-train or ride in an abusive manner.

▶ Correct mistakes rather than punish your horse.

▶ Make the show a place for competing and not for training.

▶ Address performance issues immediately rather than waiting for them to be exacerbated.

Proper Nourishment

▶ Provide enough quality feed to maintain a performance horse.

▶ Add vitamins and supplements to help your horse perform at a peak level, but not in a manner that can cause harm.

▶ Avoid substances that mask pain or illness.

▶ Keep fluid levels adequate during training and performance.

Appropriate Health Care

▶ Give immediate attention to any health issues or lamenesses.

▶ Administer proper doses of medication and keep a strict preventive medicine program with regular vaccinations and deworming.

▶ Maintain feet with regular visits from the farrier.

CARING FOR THE HORSE'S BODY

Just like any athlete, your horse's body needs to be kept

in top physical condition so that he can perform at his prime. His hooves, muscles, and joints all require regular attention.

Hooves

There's an old saying, "No hoof, no horse," and it's especially pertinent to the reining horse: The required physical maneuvers risk damage from a simple misstep and the constant concussion of performing at high speeds can cause added stress.

The horse's sliding plates must be attached securely to his well-maintained feet. Horses can rip off their shoes when the shoes are too long or not attached properly. A sliding plate is slightly oblong, with several inches (the "trailer," see p. 41) sticking out past the hoof. By simply stepping on the trailer, the horse can tear his shoe off—and parts of his hoof with it.

The horse's foot grows approximately ¼ inch each month, so your horse will need a trim and his shoes reset or new shoes put on every five to six weeks. Shoes usually need to be replaced about once every three shoeings, depending on the footing where you ride and how "hard" and frequently your horse is stopping. If you do a lot of stopping on harder ground, the shoes will get too thin to be of much use.

Your farrier should be experienced shoeing a reining horse. A good farrier knows that the "angle" made by a horse's foot to the ground needs to match the other angles in the rest of his body—in particular, the angle of his pastern. When trimming leaves the foot and pastern misaligned, you end up with a sore horse because he is not "balanced" during his work.

Healthy feet are moist so that they can hold the horseshoe nails in place. When feet are too dry they chip and crack easily. If your horse loses shoes on a regular basis, discuss the situation with your farrier; you may need to consider supplementing his feed with something such as Farrier's Formula™, which has vitamins and minerals specially formulated for healthy hooves.

Muscles and Conditioning

Your horse's muscles must be built up and strengthened to absorb the stresses of showing and training. You wouldn't consider running a marathon with just a couple of weeks training, so you should not expect your horse to!

Consistent riding to the point where your horse breaks a sweat will begin to build his muscles and his endurance. Specific exercises that involve collection and flexibility will help to build his abdominal muscles as well as his topline so that he has the ability to "round" his back and lift up his belly, creating the "frame" necessary to perform the maneuvers (see p. 67). While specific training exercises for these purposes are outside the scope of this book, there are some great references out there, such as *Reining Essentials* by Sandy Collier with Jennifer Forsberg Meyer (Trafalgar Square Books, 2008).

To understand your horse's muscle endurance, you have to understand how muscles work. The muscular system in your horse makes up the largest mass of tissue and comprises not just the outer "working" muscles, but his stomach, intestines, and organs. Your horse's body uses energy derived from glycogen and fat stores—either with oxygen (*aerobic metabolism*) or without it (*anaerobic metabolism*). Aerobic metabolism allows only for slow production of energy, so when activity demands sudden "bursts" of high intensity work, energy is generated more rapidly via anaerobic metabolism. A horse's body is built to allow for intense efforts of short duration within the realm of anaerobic metabolism. However, when your horse cannot breathe in the oxygen necessary for the activity—say, when your horse isn't properly conditioned and you are galloping your second, fast circle in a reining pattern—then the byproduct called lactic acid is released. Lactic acid causes muscle fatigue and therefore poor performance. It is important that anaerobic activity during training is broken up by adequate numbers of rest breaks and proper hydration.

Because your horse's muscles need glycogen or fatty acids to "burn," you must feed him a balanced diet to ensure he maintains his weight and health during training. Again, entire books are based on this topic. To determine your individual horse's diet requirements, it is best that you speak with your veterinarian. What you feed will be determined by your horse's current body condition, his ideal condition, and training and showing schedule.

Joints

The joints of your horse are under a great deal of stress, even with normal wear and tear. In the sport of reining,

Common Lameness in the Hock

Bog Spavin   Swelling in the top joint, the tibiotarsal.
Bone Spavin   Swelling in the lower two joints.

Definition: Synovial Joint

Synovial joints have fluid-filled capsules between the articulating (moving) bones. These joints have a greater range of motion than fibrous joints (in skulls) or cartilaginous joints (the pelvis or vertebrae). Synovial joints in the horse include the hock, stifle, knee, and pastern, and are stabilized with fibrous joint capsules and ligaments.

Seasonal Training

If you live in the north and have scheduled "downtime" during winter months when the weather is a factor, you may be able to get away with riding once or twice a week to be sure neither you nor your horse falls completely out of shape. However, in the summer, ride as much as possible to keep in "show shape." Your horse is an athlete and needs to be in prime physical condition for performing the strenuous athletic reining maneuvers.

you ask your horse to perform complicated maneuvers, and the opportunity for injury is common.

The *hocks* take the brunt of the work, as they are involved in every single maneuver. The hock is made up of four joints called the *tibiotarsal,* the *proximal inter-tarsal, distal inter-tarsal,* and *tarso-metatarsal* joints, but it is the first that provides for the majority of the movement.

The *stifle* is the largest synovial joint in the horse's body surrounded by a lot of soft structures and ligaments. It is comparable to the human knee, and when an injury occurs there, damage can often be seen in the adjacent structures.

Keeping your horse's joints healthy depends on your maintaining his good physical condition while paying close attention to stressors on the hock. Annual X-rays can help you keep abreast of any issues.

SCHEDULED DOWNTIME

An overlooked component of horse health is scheduled downtime. It is common for reiners to give their horses as much as two months off a year with no riding at all. In California and other warm states, you can show year round, but in Canada, competitors tend to show between March and November. This means that your horse may have longer time off the farther north you live because there are fewer show months in the year.

The amount of downtime you give your horse may also depend on what type of horse you have. If he is experienced and needs very little training to stay sharp, you will not need to ride him as much as a less experienced or high maintenance horse (especially during downtime). Note: if he's an "easy keeper," meaning he can gain weight easily, time off might have to also include an off-season diet.

GROOMING

Performing in a sport with rustic cowboy roots, you might think that it wouldn't matter what a reining horse looks like, as long as he can get the job done. This is not so. Reiners are very particular about grooming their horses, especially manes and tails. These require upkeep all year long, not just during the show season (figs. 5.1 A & B).

Manes

The mane should be long and flowing: no thinning or pulling as the thicker the better. To keep it long and tangle-free, many owners will leave it in thick braids (fig. 5.2). These are not braided tightly and are not uncomfortable but simply keep the mane out of the way and untangled. Before going to a show, they remove the braids, wash the mane, let it dry straight, and braid it again. Doing the braids too soon after washing makes the mane kinky, which is undesirable. A shine enhancer or leave-in conditioner (there are many varieties to be found at tack stores) is often sprayed along the entire mane so that the braid has some flexibility. Note: when your horse has a thinner mane, you may not want to leave braids in for too long as strand breakage may occur.

To keep your horse's mane clean, you might want your horse to wear a "slinky." These spandex sleeves go over the horse's head and neck (with holes for muzzle,

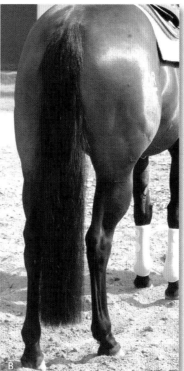

5.2 *Braids are commonly used to keep the mane from getting tangled. They should be loose and comfortable for the horse, and they must be re-braided regularly.*

5.1 A & B *The mane and tail of a reining horse are the owner's pride and joy. Both should be long, thick, and tangle-free.*

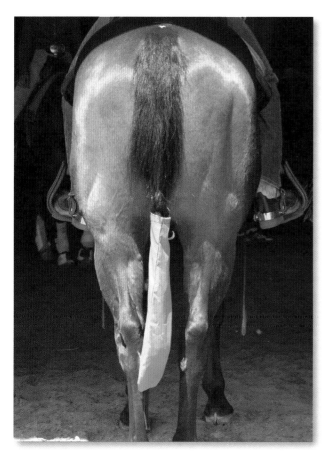

5.3 *A tailbag can help keep your horse's tail free from manure and dirt, and prevent breakage.*

eyes, and ears) and often have a belly band that fastens around the girth line. Not only do they keep an unruly mane clean and tamed, they prevent hair from being rubbed out or caught.

Because a horse sweats along his neck while working, the skin at the root of the mane can get dirty and stay moist and cause fungal growth resulting in hair loss or thinning. Keep fungus at bay with monthly applications of tea tree oil spray or a diluted Listerine® spray (one part water, one part Listerine) along the crest of his neck.

Tails

A long, thick, and flowing tail is the preferred style in a reining horse. And, just like the mane, many riders maintain their horse's healthy tail by washing it once a week and braiding it. You can also buy "tail bags" to prevent stains, ripped hair, or damage (fig. 5.3). Some types of tail bags include yarn or string attachments to help with fly control.

Many a tail has been thinned considerably by over-zealous backing-up during training or reining runs as the horse steps on his own tail. You can actually hear spectators groan when they see a large chunk pulled

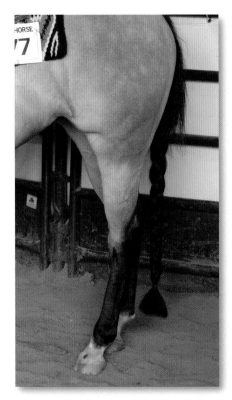

5.4 *By trimming the horse's tail to fetlock height, you can prevent it from being stepped on during back-ups. Here it is braided to keep it clean prior to entering the show pen.*

Easy Homemade Conditioner

1 bottle of Mane 'N Tail® Conditioner

1 jar of Lekair® Cholesterol Plus Strengthening & Conditioner (a product for humans available in drug stores)

½ bottle of Luster's® Pink® Oil Moisturizer Hair Lotion (available in drug stores)

Mix together. After bathing your horse, put a handful in a bucket, fill with warm water, and sponge all over your horse, including his mane and tail. Leave on for several minutes and rinse out. The results are amazing and the cost is cheap! One batch should last one horse the duration of an average show season.

out during a run, not just because it may have hurt the horse, but also because they know the number of man-hours that go into "tail maintenance."

For this reason, you sometimes see horses with the tail trimmed to fetlock height (fig. 5.4). This leaves several inches of room between the bottom of the tail and the ground—enough to avoid stepping on it when "in reverse."

For horses that have already experienced a tail-thinning tragedy, or for those not naturally endowed in this department, there are "false" tails made of real horse hair. You can purchase one that matches your horse's hair color and tie it into his real tail. When done properly it can be left in for several days (figs. 5.5 A–C). Of course, there have been cases where a false tail has been pulled off during a run, eliciting a few giggles from spectators.

Daily Routine

Wash your horse's mane and tail three or four times a month and always with a mild soap and conditioner. Using only conditioner and leaving out the soap every other time can help when your horse is prone to dry skin: look for dry, flaky skin on his tail bone. For shampoo and conditioner, it can be most cost effective to buy the biggest vat of mild human product that you can find at the drug store.

You do not have to brush the mane and tail each day when you have it in braids, but you should do so once a week. Remove the elastic(s) from the mane or tail and take out 1 or 2 inches of braid. Using a wide bristled comb, start from the bottom of the hair and work your way up so that you are brushing over the hair that is already tangle-free (fig. 5.7). Then undo another 2 inches and repeat. By brushing from the bottom up, fewer hairs will be pulled out.

Leave-in conditioners and detanglers can be used daily. Spray a detangler on a braid before undoing it or work it into the hair with your fingers before you put the braid back in. It does not matter whether you are using human or horse products; however, generic human versions are probably the least expensive.

Clipping

Reining horses are clipped before they show for better presentation, though it is not a prerequisite and

5.5 A–C   *A false tail is attached to the dock of the real tail by braiding it in with the horse's natural hair (A). When the hair is smoothed over, you should not be able to tell it is there (B) To help the false tail lie flat along the bone, wind a polo wrap around it during warm-up (C), but don't forget to remove it before you enter the show pen.*

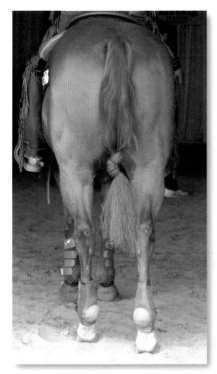

5.6   *A tail knot is a popular way to keep the tail off the ground during the warm-up just prior to a class. This prevents it from getting dirty during stops or stepped on during back-ups.*

5.7   *Brush your horse's tail from the bottom up to prevent tangling and breakage.*

Quick How-To: Clipping the Ears

Fold the sides of the horse's ear together so that they are touching (A) and move the clippers down the two sides at the same time (B). Keep the clippers flat against the ear, not pointing into it. Once the large tufts have been taken care of, you can try to get some of the hair inside the ear (C). Do not move too quickly or push the clippers in too deeply as your horse's ear is extremely sensitive. Move the clippers with the contour of the ears.

does not need to be done all year long. Get your horse accustomed to the clippers well in advance of your first show. If you wait until the day before, you may run into trouble.

Before you begin, make sure that your clipper blades have been sharpened. Dull blades can pull the hairs, causing your horse pain and not making him very predisposed to being clipped.

Begin with the muzzle, moving the clippers over the thick muzzle hairs. Next, the big guard hairs around the eyes (not the eyelashes). It can help to lay a finger across your horse's eyelid to encourage him to keep his eye closed. Because this means he can't see anything on the side you are on, your horse must really trust you.

Then clip the underside of the jaw and along the jaw bones. Allow the clippers to move along the natural contour of the jaw, laying them flat on his jaw rather than pointing toward it. Feeling the clippers along bone can be jarring for a horse as it reverberates and can cause uncomfortable sensations.

When clipping the ears, move slowly and do not try to do more than your horse is comfortable with. Better to have slightly hairy ears than ears with chunks

of hair missing. Over time your horse will become more accustomed to this process (see sidebar).

Some reiners clip their horse's front legs, especially in the early months of the year, when the hair is long. Do not clip the hind legs as the hair there can prove to be a protective element during sliding stops. If the area at the back of the fetlock is clipped and you do not have skid boots on, your horse can incur abrasions during stops.

At a Show

Keeping your horse clean at the show will save time and embarrassment. No one wants to show a horse with a big manure stain on his hip. And if you have been around horses for any length of time, you will know that the lighter color the horse, the more attracted he is to a pile of manure!

Have at least two show blankets or sheets to put on your horse while at the show. A light nylon sheet with a belly band and hood will keep most of the dirt off him for the show's duration. Using a slinky keeps the hay and straw or shavings out of his mane.

5.9   *When at a show, bathe your horse a couple times a day. Use mild soap and remember to unbraid manes and tails before bathing to prevent "crimping."*

5.10   *It is useful to have a "pit crew" to help you get your horse ready for the show pen.*

6 Tack and Equipment

Equipment used in reining can be as specialized as you'd like it to be. Just as with any other Western discipline, there are saddles, bridles, and bits that have been developed specifically for the sport to make training and riding the horse easier.

THE SADDLE

You are going to be spending many hours in your saddle so it is important you get one that works for you and your horse. Just as all horses are built differently, all riders are built differently as well. What you want to find is one that first fits your horse, and second, helps you to be the best rider that you can be.

Stirrup leathers on reining saddles should move freely forward and backward and also hang straight down so that the rider's body is properly aligned when seated (see p. 60). The ear should be in line with the shoulder, the shoulder in line with the hips, and the legs should hang naturally, not forced forward or backward to fit in the stirrup.

The horn and swells on the saddle should be low, allowing for lateral hand movement. The cantle of the saddle is also usually low and the seat deep, allowing the rider maximum room for the hip movement needed for a proper sliding stop.

Choose a seat width that gives your legs enough room to move during a sliding stop. While you may feel a little more secure in a saddle that "hugs" you and keeps you seated, you won't feel very comfortable when your thighs are black and blue from repeated contact with the swells on your saddle.

Most saddles found in tack shops are called "production saddles." There are dozens of saddles made specifically for reining horses. Try out lots of them until you find one that fits both you and your horse.

Successful trainers frequently have a custom-made saddle they use successfully then patent its pattern so that you can buy one of "their" saddles.

Form vs. Function

Styles of saddles go in and out of fashion: square or round skirt corners, flower or basket stamping, heavy silver accents to just a few conchos (figs. 6.1 A–F).

You should avoid a saddle with a lot of silver on its skirt as the added weight and stiffness can restrict the movement of your horse's shoulders or hips. During physically demanding maneuvers like the spin, sliding stop, and rollback, he needs as much freedom as he can get. The look of a saddle has never won anyone points in the show pen! As long as your saddle is safe for you and your horse and allows you to perform, it will work just fine.

6.1 A–F   *There are many different saddle styles to choose from. Plus, many parts can be custom made or specially fitted for the rider or horse. These are examples of just a few: Cutaway skirt for easier stirrup and leg movement (A); rounded skirt with minimal silver (B); rounded skirt with corner plates in silver—this is less flexible in the horse's hip area (C); basic reining saddle with a slick seat, minimal silver, and basket weave stamp (D); fancy show saddle with ornate stamping (E); seat with a front rise, which encourages the rider to sit back, and a cutaway skirt for easier leg movement (F).*

CINCHES

Many Western saddles have two cinches: one each for the front and the back. The front cinch is the most important. It is commonly made out of cotton or neoprene and can be adjusted on both ends, though the right side is left attached when the saddle is taken off the horse. Both cinches are attached to D-rings built into the saddle.

Reiners are divided as to whether or not their saddles require back (or "rear") cinches. Some believe that if a horse isn't started with a back cinch, he will buck when you put one on him. There is some wisdom to this: he may not notice it at first, but as soon as he's performed a maneuver or started loping, he may suddenly realize that it's there and object!

However, a back cinch has a purpose. It helps to keep the saddle snug in place during reining maneuvers. (If you have always ridden with one, you can tell right away that it's missing because your saddle feels a little bit looser.)

It is imperative that when you put a back cinch on you do two things: tighten it up so that it fits properly and connect it to the front cinch with a strip of leather, tied to the cinch rings, called a latigo: you do not want

Custom-Built Saddles

There are many reasons for buying a custom saddle.

First, the saddle is fitted to your horse with the internal parts of the saddle constructed with his conformation in mind.

Second, the maker will be able to build it knowing that it will be for reining, thus creating a structure that suits the sport.

Third, you and your unique body can be taken into consideration. Men have much narrower hips than women and the majority of saddle manufacturers make saddles that fit a man's body.

What's Your Size?

Saddles come in 1-inch sizes from 12 to 17 inches. This measurement is taken from the base of the horn, straight back to the middle of the cantle.

Does the Saddle Fit Your Horse?

Stand your horse on a level surface and place your saddle pad on followed by the saddle. Ensure it is in the proper location so that the cinch hangs down at the horse's girth. Do the saddle up with two-fingers-width between the horse's elbow and the cinch (fig. 6.2).

You should be able to place no more than four fingers stacked on top of one another between the saddle pad and the withers. When you put the saddle on top of the saddle pad, lift the pad up into the gullet of the saddle so it is not stretched tight across the withers (fig. 6.3). This can create a pressure point and even damage the nerves in the area.

You should be able to comfortably fit your hand between the horse's shoulder and the saddle pad whether mounted or not. After a workout, check for any dry patches in the sweat left by the saddle on your horse's back. Dry patches around the withers or along the back indicate that the saddle is squeezing the withers and preventing sweat from being excreted. Having the wrong saddle pad can also cause this problem, which I discuss below.

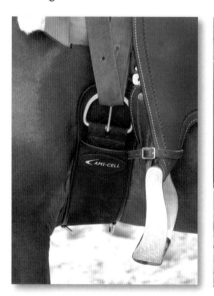

6.2　*The cinch should not restrict the horse's leg movement. There should be two-fingers-width between the elbow and the cinch.*

6.3　*This saddle pad has been lifted into the gullet to give the horse's withers room. You can see the space between the front end of the pad and the neck.*

the back cinch to dangle so a hind foot could become caught during a maneuver, nor do you want it to move farther back along the flank and irritate your horse.

THE SADDLE PAD

There are many kinds of saddle pads, all with pros and cons. If possible, try a few to see which one fits your horse best in conjunction with the saddle. If your saddle was custom-built, the maker might have suggested a pad to go with it. You know it fits your saddle and your horse

when you are not finding dry patches and can test the fit with your hands as indicated in the sidebar above.

The two most important considerations are compression and cooling. The pad should provide protection for the horse's back and allow the skin to breathe. To test a pad for compression, pinch it with your thumb and finger: when you can feel the other digit it does not have enough protection. To provide cooling, choose natural fibers or ones that wick or absorb sweat—when not removed, sweat prevents air from reaching the skin.

"Hospital felts" are the most popular pad and are made of pressed wool and synthetic fibers that give an even cushioning for the saddle. They are off-white in color and clean very well. However, when used for too long they can develop thin spots.

Gel pads come in many shapes and sizes: some with holes down the center for venting, some thin, some thick. Basically, they are neoprene or vinyl/plastic "bladders" filled with gel and do offer fairly good cushioning. However, the materials do not allow the horse's skin to breathe or absorb or wick away any moisture at all.

A wool blanket can be friendly to a horse's back because its natural fibers help keep the saddle in place, almost like a natural Velcro™. This is a popular choice for showing because of the pad's attractive look and possible color combinations. Wool blankets can be hard to clean, due to shrinkage, but a show pad does not need to be cleaned as often as your regular pad since it is only used once in a while. The only downside is cost—expect to pay more than $100 for a good one. Some may cost well over $200 including leather and silver add-ons. You do not require this type of pad to be a successful competitor. It's better to spend the money on a few extra lessons.

BRIDLES AND BITS

A bridle is the term used for the entire contraption when a bit and headstall are attached. There is little difference between Western headstalls, all have a leather strap that attaches to the cheekpiece of the bit, goes over the horse's head (behind the ears) and attaches to the other cheekpiece. Some have a leather strip going across the forehead called a browband, others have a leather loop over one or two ears. You can choose any style as long as it has a chin or curb strap made of either leather or linked chains that lie flat against your horse's chin.

However, when it comes to bits, the selection is just as wide, but the choice can make a much bigger difference to your horse. A horse's mouth is much more individual than you may think, considering that horses' heads are structurally similar. However, your horse may have a flat palate or a shallow jaw and may prefer one bit over another. When you purchase a horse, always ask what type of bit the horse prefers.

When choosing a bit, know how it works. There are specific points in a horse's mouth and face that the bit "works" on: the palate; tongue; bars (also called the inter-

6.4　*The snaffle bit should fit in your horse's mouth so that there is almost a wrinkle in the corner of the mouth.*

dental space); curb area (the dent under his chin) for leverage bits (see p. 38) with a curb strap or chain; and cheeks.

A snaffle bit has round cheekpieces that are most often shaped like a circle, oval, or a "D" and can be loose (allowing the mouthpiece to slide) or fixed. When a rein pulls on a ring, the mouthpiece, which is hinged in the middle, presses on the bars of the mouth and the tongue (fig. 6.4). There is often a leather chin strap that is attached to the rings and hangs loosely under the chin. Its function is to keep the bit from slipping through the mouth and therefore it does not need to be tight. The snaffle is ridden with two hands; however, it is legally acceptable in the show pen to ride with one hand as long as you don't change to two hands halfway through the pattern.

Parts of a Bit

Mouthpiece: The metal part that rests inside the horse's mouth, on his tongue.

Cheekpiece: The metal part on the outside of the mouth.

Port: The raised portion in the center of the mouthpiece seen on shanked bits.

Roller: A cylinder attached to the mouthpiece—most often on a shanked bit—that rolls with the movement of the tongue.

What Are Bits Made Of?

Your horse may have a preference of not only a bit style, but the metal, too:

Stainless steel is the most common, and is shiny and easy to clean, but some horses do not like the taste.

Sweet iron is designed to rust as some horses like the flavor it produces.

Copper encourages the production of saliva, which keeps the horse's mouth "soft."

Inlay and combinations are most often made of stainless steel or sweet iron with copper inlayed in vertical strips. There may also be an add-on such as a roller or extra joint made of copper.

Chin and Curb Straps

A chin strap refers to a strip of leather attached to a bit that sits behind the chin and is used with snaffle bits. A curb strap is a flat chain used with a shanked bit, which must be installed and used properly so that there are no twists or kinks in the chain. A twisted curb strap may be uncomfortable for your horse and will result in a "no score" in the show pen.

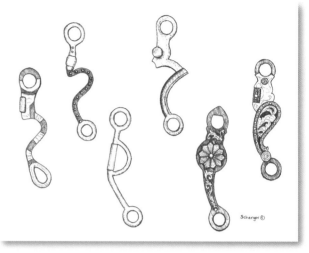

6.5 *There are a variety of shank styles to choose from when riding in a shanked bit.*

A shanked bit is called this because it has a metal shank attached to the mouthpiece and the rein is attached to the bottom of the shank (fig. 6.5). It provides leverage so a small pull on the rein results in greater pressure inside the mouth. Shanked bits can have hinged mouthpieces that work on the bars and the tongue, but can also be solid with raised ports that take some pressure off the tongue and put it on the roof of the mouth.

A shanked bit is used in combination with a metal curb strap (see sidebar) that puts pressure on the curb area behind the chin when the bit is "engaged." This curb strap often has two leather "keepers" or buckles with a chain laid flat in between. Shanked bits must be ridden with one hand. Some NRHA class rules require shanked bits while others allow snaffles (see the *NRHA Handbook*).

The hackamore works on the top of the nose and the jawline and is ridden with two hands. Correct fitting of a hackamore is crucial or your horse will end up with sores on his face and jaw. It consists of a flexible, braided leather or rope bosal (the noseband), which has a core of either rawhide or flexible cable—no rigid material allowed. At the cheek the bosal must be at least 3/4-inch wide.

The hackamore's use confounds most new reiners and because of this are used most often by experienced horsemen. You have a lot less control over a horse unless he has had training to be ridden in one, and it can feel a lot like trying to ride a horse in a halter. You

6.6 *You should be able to fit two fingers between the chin and the curb strap.*

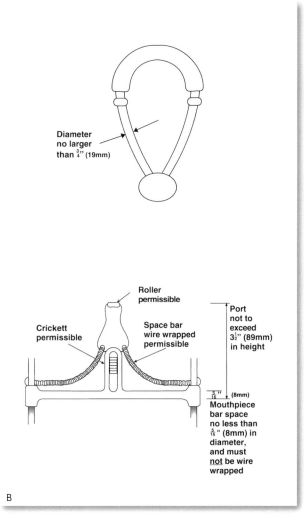

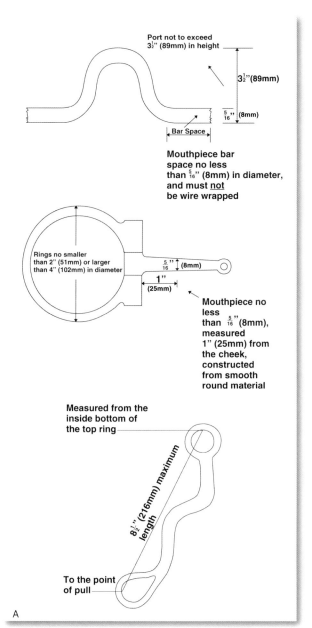

6.7 A & B *The NRHA has specific guidelines for the thickness and type of bit you use (A) as well as the type of port and bosal you can use (B).*

Illegal Equipment

Bosal with any rigid material inside (metal, wire rods)

Horsehair bosal

Mechanical hackamore

Snaffles with rings larger than 4 inches or smaller than 2 inches

Snaffles thinner than 5/16 inch or thicker than 1 inch in diameter, measured 1 inch from the cheek

Bit with a shank longer than 8½ inches

Mouthpieces wrapped with anything

Ports higher than 3½ inches

Curb chains with any twists or kinks

Snaffles with curb chains rather than curb straps

6.8 *The bosal should be fitted correctly to your horse's face so that it does not rub.*

need to steer him with a combination of neck reining and a series of "bumps" that tell him where you want him to go. It is very easy to teach a horse to become numb to these "bumps," and this can lead to a dangerous situation with no control over direction.

REINS

There are three types of reins you can use: split, romal, and mecate.

Split reins are used with a snaffle or shanked bit. They are the reins most commonly seen and are simply two long strips of leather attached to each side of the bit and held with either one or two hands. They are not fastened together in any way.

Romals are leather reins with rawhide braiding on them. They are attached to the bit in the same fashion as split reins and fastened together halfway down their length, forming a "Y" with a long tail. You hold these reins one-handed. Your guiding (or steering) hand (nor-

mally the left) holds the reins in front of the "Y" joint. Your other hand holds the tail but must not guide your horse or move to adjust the length of your reins or you will receive a "zero" penalty mark in the show pen.

A mecate rein made of horsehair, mohair, or marine-grade rope is a rein used with a hackamore or a snaffle bit and attached to the bit with slobber straps (thick leather straps). It is approximately 20 feet long, but you actually use less than half this length, and the rest usually is attached to your saddle or tucked into your belt. The use of the mecate is generally a personal preference as it has an old-time look to it.

LEG PROTECTION

Your horse's legs are the moving parts of his machine and the tendons, ligaments, and bones can be injured from long-term repetitive strains or impact injuries. To protect and support all four of his legs, you can either wrap them with a bandage or polo wrap (see p. 42 for instructions) or use some type of boot, or both.

Splint boots are generally made with leather or a synthetic material and held onto your horse's lower front legs with Velcro™. They protect the inside of your horse's leg between the knee and the fetlock with thick leather. This is the area most commonly injured during spins (fig. 6.9).

Another type of splint boot, called a "sport medicine boot" is less structured and made of neoprene on the inside and a Velcro-like material on the outside. It provides protection from concussive injury on the inside of the front leg with thick neoprene padding and also supports the ligaments by cupping the fetlock with a neoprene band (fig. 6.10).

Bell boots are like thick neoprene "cones" that fasten around the pastern and protect the hoof and coronet band from injury. However, they are often used for knee protection as well (figs. 6.11 A & B). Many reiners attach a bell boot upside down above the splint boot (at the top of the cannon bone, below the knee) so that it covers the knee. Actual knee boots do exist. They are flexible, unstructured boots generally made with neoprene and fastened with Velcro or built into a combination boot that protects the leg from fetlock to knee.

Skid boots are worn on the back legs and attach above and below the fetlock with leather straps (figs. 6.12 A & B). Protecting the fetlock is a cup that can

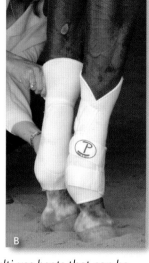

6.9 *Splint boots are popular because they are easy to apply.*

6.10 *Sport medicine boots have gained in popularity over the years for their ligament support.*

6.11 A & B *Bell boots are multi-use boots that can be used to protect the foot as shown in A or the knee as described on p. 40. The white boots in B have knee protection built in.*

6.12 A & B *Skid boots are a necessity, especially for horses that stop hard and have a tendency to dig deep into the ground.*

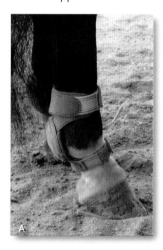

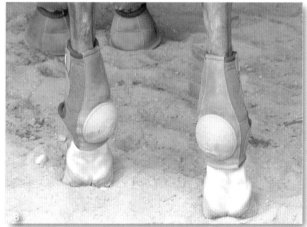

be made of leather only, or metal, or plastic wrapped in leather. When a horse stops too deep in the ground this boot protects his fetlock from a painful scrape against the base (the solid ground under the sand) of the arena floor.

SHOES AND SLIDING PLATES

Sliding plates are the specialized shoes that allow a reining horse to complete a sliding stop. They are put onto the hind feet and range from ¾ to 1½ inches in width and may have extended heels or "trailers" (the area of

the shoe that sticks out past the hoof) of a variety of lengths. The bottom of the shoe is smooth and the nail heads are "countersunk" or flush so each nail head is just a fraction below the plane of the shoe and the surface is completely flat—perfect for sliding (fig. 6.14).

If nail heads can be felt when you run your hand along the bottom of the shoe, they might catch on the ground when your horse is stopping. (Think of shoveling manure or snow and the feeling you get when your shovel scoop hits something hidden and unexpected.) The stress on the hoof as the impact pulls on the shoe and nails may also result in an increased number of lost

Polo Wrap Application

1 Hold wrap on leg with the end aligned with the cannon bone (A).

2 Wrap clockwise around and down the leg, bringing the wrap toward you and across the front of the cannon bone, tugging slightly only when you are crossing the cannon bone. Keep even tension throughout the process (B).

3 At the fetlock, angle the wrap approximately 45 degrees down (C).

4 "Cup" the wrap around the back of the fetlock (D).

5 Begin to wrap back up around the leg (E).

6 When you reach the top of the leg you should also reach the Velcro™ that is attached to the wrap. Unwrap it and fasten (F).

7 When viewed from the front, there should be an upside down V in the center of the leg (G).

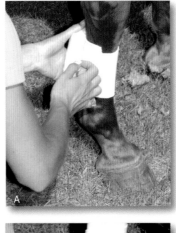

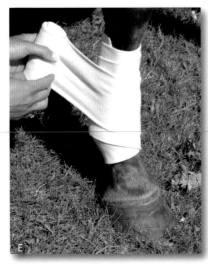
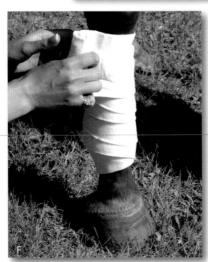
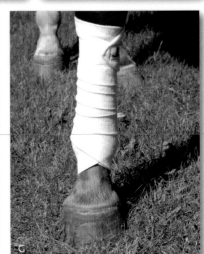

6.13 A–G *Polo wraps can be used for both tendon and ligament support and protection. They must be put on correctly or they may cause pressure-point injuries to the tendon.*

shoes as the nails eventually loosen in the hoof. Your farrier should always use a tool (called a rasp) to shave off the part of the nail sticking out. An inexperienced farrier may not realize the importance of this or may even believe that your horse will simply wear the nail heads down by stopping enough times.

Just as with any shoe, the sliding plate must be fit to the horse's feet. There are ways to customize these shoes to help a reining horse stop better. Normally, the trailers are about an inch long. Some horses spread their hind feet wide when they stop, or stop crookedly. A farrier well-versed in shoeing the reining horse can make adjustments in width of the shoe and length of the trailers to help the horse stop correctly, even having one trailer longer than the other.

After you have made a sliding stop, turn around and look at the marks your horse has left behind. They should consist of two straight, parallel lines. When there are breaks or inconsistencies in the lines, then your horse may be having difficulty holding himself "in the ground." This could mean that a shoe is loose or that it, or a nail head, is catching on the ground.

While most horse owners will put regular horse shoes on the front feet, they are not required to perform reining maneuvers.

What to Do when You Lose a Shoe

Inspect your horse's shoes before each ride to ensure that the nails are holding and a shoe is not loose. When you wiggle the shoe slightly, your horse's foot should wiggle with it and there should be no gaps between foot and shoe.

However, due to the physical maneuvers in reining, a horse can step on a trailer and pull off his own shoe.

6.14   *The sliding plate has nails that are flush with the shoe so that they do not interfere with stopping.*

Just frolicking in the paddock can result in shoes being lost forever. Sliding plates are notoriously "sucked off" by thick, heavy mud.

When your horse loses a shoe, don't ride him until it is put back on or replaced. You might consider riding him slowly and just not saying "Whoa" (the cue for a sliding stop—not just any stop), but it is unsafe. Ask your farrier to come out right away (or if you are at a show, visit the show farrier) or failing a replacement, have someone safely remove the other sliding plate so he has an equal grip. A final word of warning: Do not ever ask a trained reining horse to stop without sliding plates—he may hurt himself trying to do so.

7 Looking the Part: Show Clothes

Now we come to the shopaholic-horseaholic hybrid's favorite chapter. Here you will find topics on purchasing and coordinating show clothes. Though the men reading may want to skip ahead to more "important" chapters, please, stay with me—in the world of reining, dressing the part is important.

Shawn Flarida, the NRHA's first Three-Million-Dollar rider and All-Time Leading Money Earner, is often referred to as "the man in green" because he wears only green shirts when showing (fig. 7.1). (His Web address is even www.thegreenshirt.com!) Since he cares about what *he* looks like, maybe *you* should, too.

WESTERN SHOWING ATTIRE

There are a few rules outlined in the *NRHA Handbook*, "Section L," for correct attire. It states: "It is mandatory for all riders to use appropriate Western tack and Western attire while showing; this would include a long sleeved shirt, Western hat or safety helmet, boots, Western saddle, and Western bridle."

The American Quarter Horse Association (AQHA) has more specific guidelines: "...appropriate Western attire is required, which includes pants (slacks, trousers, jeans, etc.) long sleeves and collar (band, standup, tuxedo, etc.), Western hat, and cowboy boots." In addition it is noted that "judges, at their discretion, may authorize adjustments to attire due to weather-related conditions" (2007 AQHA Show Rules Section 445).

To avoid any confusion, look to competitors that have been in the show pen for many years. Styles for the Professional or Non Pro rider are the same: women wear well-fitting, stylish, and respectful attire, and men wear crisp, neat, and subdued items.

SHIRTS

Women's Shirts Dressing "Western" isn't just long-sleeved shirts with a collar—at least not any more (figs. 7.2 A–D). Now, it includes shirts with three collar styles: traditional dress, or Western collar, as seen on most men's shirts; Mandarin, band, buckaroo, or tuxedo; or mock turtleneck. Women may also wear a "slinky," which is a spandex top that has a mock turtleneck collar. It tucks into your pants and may have sparkles or sequins. It may be worn alone, or paired with a vest or cropped jacket.

Men's Shirts Choose a nice, pressed, Western shirt with any collar type (traditional dress or Western collar, Mandarin, band, buckaroo, or tuxedo), tucked neatly into your jeans and puffed out slightly (fig. 7.3). You may wear a vest on top if you choose.

7.1   *Shawn Flarida, the NRHA's All-Time Leading Money Earner, has become known for the green shirts he competes in.*

THE CLASSIC STYLE

All fashion fads appear in the show pen, but they never supersede classic styles. For men and women alike, a clean, pressed, Western shirt tucked neatly into jeans will never go out of style.

"Black fringed suede chaps and a high-quality black felt hat are the classic items that are the 'bones' of many show wardrobes," says Suzi Drnec, President of Hobby Horse Clothing Company "They can be slightly altered to stay trendy, but fine quality hats and chaps will give years and years of service."

"Evergreen" choices for women are, in addition to hat and chaps, a tailored vest that matches the chaps in color and texture to pair with the "blouse of the moment," and large, colorful saddle blankets that

Attire Exceptions

The American Quarter Horse Association (AQHA) allows exceptions to its Western-attire regulations for reasons of religion or physical handicap. However, you must file a written request and receive approval prior to competition.

The American Paint Horse Association (APHA) specifies that your pants must be ankle length or longer, but also makes exception for religious reasons. APHA judges may also authorize adjustments to attire due to weather-related conditions.

All associations allow the competitor to wear a safety helmet rather than a Western hat if they choose.

7.2 A–D   *When it comes to shirts, women have a few more style choices than men. Here you see a classic older-style Western shirt designed by Molly Sapergia (A); a slinky shirt with collar and cuffs, in both a bold pattern and a single color with sequins, by Hobby Horse Clothing Company (B & C); and a slinky shirt with collar and cuffs paired with a vest by Hobby Horse Clothing Company (D).*

For the Ladies

A word of advice for female riders: invest in a good, properly fitting bra. When you stop your horse, *all* parts of your body should stop at the same time.

7.4   *A slinky (a form-fitting spandex shirt with a mock turtleneck collar) can be worn alone or with a vest.*

7.3   *Men generally show in clean, pressed, Western shirts with a traditional collar.*

Color Coordination Chart

The biggest influence on the colors you choose for your show clothes will not be your own coloring, but that of your horse. When choosing a wardrobe, match:

► Hat and chaps
► Boots and belt
► Shirt and saddle pad
► Jeans and chaps (although blue jeans are always appropriate)

And *everything* should match the color of your horse.

7.5 *A wonderful tool from Hobby Horse Clothing Company is its horse-coordination chart. Use it as a basic fashion guide when choosing your show wardrobe.*

7.6 A & B "Chaps should hang from your waist, not your hips. They should fit snugly at the top and should be fitted to the knee," says Suzi Drnec, President of Hobby Horse Clothing Company. The color can be chosen to match your horse, and they come in a variety of styles, including suede (A), leather, or a mixture of materials with silver adornment (B).

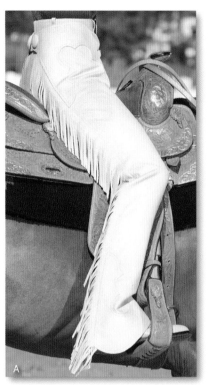 

visually pull horse and rider together as a team. For men, a starched, tailored shirt in white or solid color that works with any saddle blanket.

Some of the pieces to think about:

Vests A great choice for most women are show vests worn over shirts or slinkies. "They are much more flattering on many women than fitted stretch blouses that reveal our 'table muscle' area at the waist!" says Drnec. As well, they can be paired with different slinkies to create brand new looks, which is why they fit into the evergreen category.

Belts Most riders wear a belt that matches the color of their boots; however, you may color coordinate with the rest of your outfit. Belt buckles are a coveted item for reiners because they are often awarded as show prizes and are seen as marks of accomplishment. Be warned, though—do not wear one that is too big or garish; one that is the size of your fist is a good size to start with. Alternatively, you can wear a nice buckle set, which is an ornate buckle and clip in a semi-circle with additional silver pieces used as a keeper and as a clip on the tail of the belt.

Chaps Pronounced "shaps," they are made of either leather or suede, usually include fringe down the leg, and are worn over pants or jeans (figs. 7.6 A & B). Generally, chaps should be coordinated with the color of your hat. They are optional, but wearing them gives you a more polished and professional look, helping you present more appealing slim lines and contours and an overall polished appearance. They have practical applications, too. They help to hold you in the saddle and provide an extra feeling of security.

If possible, have them professionally fit by a chap maker who can build them to an exact fit and may suggest current and classic styles. You can tell your chaps fit when they do not have wrinkles as you stand, but you are able to lift your leg up to the stirrup with little effort. Once in the saddle, the bottom hem of the chaps should rest on the top of your foot while the fringe (if you have it) should hang about 6 inches past your heel.

Jeans Blue or black jeans are the most popular choice and you have several brand names to choose from including Wrangler™, Cinch™, Cruel Girl™, and Rockies™. You should choose jeans that are made specifically for riding because the thickest seam is on the outside of the leg, whereas most "fashion jeans" have that seam on the inside. Also, riding jeans are constructed with heavier rivets to withstand rough use.

ACCESSORIES

Jewelry Earrings and necklaces are popular adornments in and out of the show pen, as any fashion magazine will attest. When in the show pen, there are a few rules to make sure your jewelry does not detract from the overall picture you are presenting.

No jewelry on the wrists. It isn't expressly forbidden, but having shiny jewelry will draw attention to your hand movements. If you are wearing a necklace or earrings, make sure they are heavy enough so they don't flop or sway while you are riding.

Neck Ties An accessory trend that is making its transition from other Western sports and into the reining pen is the neck tie. Not the "normal" style neck tie, but rather a classic throwback to the Roy Rogers and Dale Evans era: the silk tie with a knot in the middle and the ends no more than a few inches long (see figs. 7.7 A & C).

HAT OR HELMET

A cowboy hat or safety helmet must be worn when showing. The classic cowboy hat is one of the defining items in your wardrobe. Cowboy hats come in either felt or straw. (Unofficially, a felt hat is appropriate year round while straw is worn only during the summer. When you live or show horses in a wet climate, you are better off with a felt hat. The properties of felt resist and shed water while straw hats retain it and swell when too wet.) Hats are graded based on a number of "Xs."

Felt Hats "Felt" is actually matted fur and stronger than woven materials (like straw) because it is first woven and then compressed, and the fibers run in all directions, interlocking with each other (fig. 7.8).

For felt hats the number of "Xs" is all about the amount of beaver (or rabbit) fur woven in the felt—though not on a direct ratio scale. The higher the number of "Xs" in the hat, the more beaver fur. For example,

7.7. A–C Coordination is key and choosing simple color patterns is also important. Here are three examples of well-chosen attire—clean, classic, and with the horse's color in mind.

What's My Hat Size?

To determine the size hat you wear, measure the circumference of your head at the forehead and divide that number by 3.145. Round up to the nearest quarter-inch. That is your hat size.

For example:
Head circumference = 22.5 inches
22.5 divided by 3.145 = 7.15
Hat size: 7.25 inches

How to Care for Your Hat

When you touch your hat, it should always be on the brim. Do not grab your hat by the crown.

Always set your hat down upside down and on the crown so the brim does not flatten.

To clean your hat, use a soft bristled brush or hat sponge. Brush with the nap and in a clockwise direction. For straw hats, just use the soft bristled brush.

When you get caught in the rain, allow your hat to dry without heat. Turn the sweatband inside out so you can stand your hat upright to dry. Heat will cause your hat to shrink or lose shape.

Straw hats should never get wet. The straw will swell and your hat will become permanently misshapen. Use a plastic hat cover to protect it.

Store your hat in a hatbox, and at least once every two or three years, have it professionally cleaned, blocked, and reshaped. Make sure your straw hat is stored properly during the off-season.

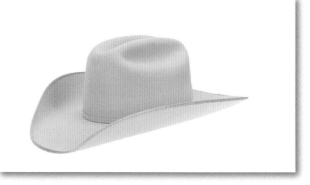

7.8   *A properly shaped hat makes you look professional and well turned out. A felt hat like this can be worn year round.*

a hat marked 5X has no beaver at all, and is all rabbit; a 10X hat is 50 percent rabbit and 50 percent beaver, and a 100X hat is 100 percent beaver.

Straw Hats   These are made of woven straw and are also graded with "Xs," which refer to the quality of the straw and how tight the weave.

For both felt and straw hats, costs can range from $50 to more than $1,000 depending on the quality: the more "Xs", the higher the quality and price.

When it comes to choosing your cowboy hat, you will want to have one that looks good on you. Keep in mind these simple tips:

▶ The smaller you are, the smaller your hat should be—you don't want to appear "overwhelmed" by your hat. Choose a hat with a small brim and small crown. If you want to appear taller, choose a hat with a higher crown, but with a slope crease.

▶ If you are taller, choose a hat with a shorter crown and a wider brim to cut down on your height, but without appearing as though you have a bowler on your head.

The shape of your face will also factor in to the type of hat you should wear:

▶ Long face: stay away from narrow brims.

▶ Round face: choose a higher crown and an oval brim.

▶ Square face: choose a shorter crown with a slope crease.

▶ Oval face: anything goes!

Be sure to have your hat shaped so it is correctly fit to your head, this can often be done at the point of purchase. Hat manufacturers, tack stores employees, or older horsemen may have this skill, or you can ship your hat with a photo of your face and head measurement to a "hat doctor" (see sidebar).

Safety Helmets When you compete in a Western performance sport like reining you will see some safety helmets in the show pen, or at home when practicing. Small, regional associations may require those under the age of 18 to wear a hard hat, but most do not. The Western horse sport industry has been notoriously slow in regulating hard hat use during competition. To help encourage their use, manufacturers have made helmets that look like cowboy hats.

BOOTS

When showing, you really can't go wrong if you just wear cowboy boots. It is best to get something that is safe, comfortable, and appropriate for showing (has a heel, and can be polished and cleaned easily). Many reiners have a pair of boots that they ride in daily, and another for shows.

Your boots should be muted in color, either black or brown. They should compliment your chaps, unless you are trying to make a colorful statement. For safety, you must have boots with a heel to prevent your foot from slipping through the stirrup during a fall. Barn shoes and boots without heels do not offer this protection.

GETTING STARTED

Suzi Drnec, one of the top names in Western show clothes for many years, suggests rookies take a conservative approach to their first few show outfits and add more dazzle and flair as they move up the competitive ladder.

"A 'get-started outfit' depends on the level where you begin," says Drnec. "If it's at a local level, the

Hat Help from Hat Doctors

The One Hat Doctor
Warrensburg, MO (USA)
660.422.HATS (4287)
www.the1hatdoctor.com

The Hat Doctor
Langdon, AB (Canada)
403.936.5090

Care of Show Attire

Show clothes are expensive so it behooves you to take care of your outfit. Your hat should be kept safe from dirt and damage as described in the sidebar on p. 50. Your boots and clothing should be cleaned after use and stored in boot and garment bags.

rider can often get by without wearing chaps, which is a big savings. My suggestion overall is to always buy the best within your budget, to use coordinating colors in shirts/blouses and saddle blankets for visual appeal, and to make sure things fit: neither too loose nor too tight.

"You can also consider one base color and one accent color. For example, black chaps, hat, and boots with a red saddle blanket and blouse is simple but stunning. You can build a wardrobe of additional pieces as necessary, but retain those basic items.

"The key to dressing for the show pen is twofold. Firstly, you want to look serious about your job and convey a sense of professionalism and confidence. Second, you should be comfortable with your attire. NRHA rules for attire allow everything from jeans and a long-sleeved shirt to expensive chaps and ornate outfits (sequins, glitter, slinkies, and vests). Never be concerned that you can't afford expensive chaps, hats, or show clothes—you don't need fancy clothes to show your horse, but you should always be neatly attired."

Look Great for Less Money

Associations that cater to youths and amateurs can be a great place to find used show clothes. Some place a rack near the show office to house show shirts, chaps, and hats that are for sale by other riders.

Pair up with another rider in your barn who is of the same size. You can share show shirts so that you have a variety of choices.

Choose neutral colors for your basic items, such as your shirt or slinky, chaps, and hat. Then add one other item at a time as you can afford it.

KEEPING CLEAN AT THE SHOW

If you have been around horses for any length of time, you know that it can be hard to keep clean—even more so when you are distracted by the busy, stressful show environment. It's right before your run that your horse will suddenly need to rub his head on your arm or try to wipe his nose on your leg.

Limit the chances of dirt and slobber on your shirt by saddling and prepping your horse before you get dressed in your show clothes. Keep a light jacket on hand to wear while warming up, and take it off only when mounted and ready to go into the show pen. (Make sure you horse is okay with you doing this—light windbreakers or jackets can make scary noises!) Have someone to help you clean up your horse before you enter your class. This keeps mounting and dismounting to the minimum.

8 Judging and Scoring

Now that I have covered the basics of reining, I'll discuss the competition itself.

For the rookie reiner, one of the most confusing aspects of the sport is the way it is scored. However, once you understand the basic concept, it makes a lot of sense. When you walk into the show pen, you start with a score of 70, no matter who you are or what kind of horse you are riding. There are two factors that can change this score: maneuver scores and penalties. It is important that you understand the difference between the two.

Each maneuver performed gets a *maneuver score* (for details, see right). These scores are awarded in ½-point increments up or down—"plus" or "minus" points—based on how well the horse performs.

During the run, you may incur *penalty points* (for details, see p. 55). These range from ½-point to 5-point penalties. They are not referred to as plus or minus points in order to distinguish them from the maneuver scores. Penalties can occur during maneuvers, but are marked separately from the maneuver itself. For example, you could have a set of left spins that marks a + ½ (said, "plus half") but incur a penalty mark of 1 point due to an overspin.

At the end of the run, maneuver scores are added up and penalties points are subtracted for a total score.

There is one common penalty that every reiner tries to avoid: the "zero." When you receive a penalty of "0," it means that your final run score is "0": it negates all other maneuver scores and penalty points.

MANEUVER SCORES

The maneuver scores have a specific quality they are supposed to reflect. A + ½ ("plus half") maneuver score on a set of left circles should be the same maneuver from a quality standpoint (i.e., "good") in California as it is in New York. (See p. 55 for descriptions of qualities needed for a good score).

+ 1½	Excellent
+1	Very good
+ ½	Good
0	Correct, no degree of difficulty
- ½	Poor
-1	Very poor
-1½	Extremely Poor

Each maneuver in a pattern is assessed by the judge in the following order:

1   Is the maneuver on pattern?

2   Is the maneuver correct?

3   Is there a degree of difficulty?

Being *on pattern* means that you have not deviated from the set maneuver in any way and the judge moves on to the second criterion. When you are *not* on pattern, you are given a "0" penalty and you have "zeroed" your run.

When you perform the maneuver *correctly* you will get, at the very least, a minimum of a "0" maneuver score. When it is not technically correct, the score will move into the *minus* territory.

For example, during a spin, one hind foot must be planted and the horse must spin around it (see p. 72). If the horse does this incorrectly by moving the hind feet too much, the maneuver may not be quite technically correct, but you have not gone "off pattern."

The *degree of difficulty* is what can increase your maneuver score. Once the judge has determined it is on pattern and correct, he will give you credit for the horse's smoothness, finesse, willing attitude, quickness, authority (confidence), and controlled speed while completing the maneuver. These are the specific qualities that the NRHA has trained judges to look for in a reining horse.

Scoring Tip for Rookies

When you start competing, do not strive for "plus" maneuver scores. It is enough to strive for a "correct" ("zero") maneuver score. Many rookie riders try to "plus" every maneuver and end up accruing penalty points because they did not focus on doing the maneuver correctly. You might assume a fast-spinning horse will score higher than a horse spinning more slowly, but it is the horse and rider that spins slowly but correctly that will be marked higher than a fast-spinning horse doing it wrong.

Remember: It is a good thing to hear a rider say "I 'zeroed' all of my maneuvers!" This is quite the opposite from "I 'zeroed' my run."

Question: *What lowers my maneuver score?*

The following examples may contribute to a lower maneuver score, but would not be considered penalties:

▶   Horse looks unwilling: pinning ears, shaking head, resistant to the reins.

▶   Rider or horse pulling too hard on the reins, causing horse's mouth to gape.

▶   Rider not guiding horse through the center during circle maneuvers.

▶   Horse abruptly increases speed during the approach to the stop (increase should be gradual and steady, not sudden).

Question: *When do I increase the level of difficulty?*

An increase in difficulty can generally be summed up as performing the correct technique with increased speed, finesse, and smoothness. When you begin to rein, staying "on pattern" and correctly completing the maneuvers are difficult. Once you begin to display consistency, you can start to think about increasing the level of difficulty. You do not need to make moves look more difficult but make moves that are difficult, look easy!

1   Always ride correctly. One of the biggest mistakes that rookies make is trying to increase the difficulty before having a firm grasp on the basics. You are making this mistake when your "penalty points" are accruing faster than your "plus maneuvers." Your first goal should be to avoid penalty points in each run.

2   Master the first step. Pick your strongest maneuver and try to step it up a notch. For example, if your horse's strongest maneuver is his spin, start the spin with minimal cues, perform four spins of increasing speed, then stop the spin with solid accuracy. Work on getting better at your best maneuver.

3   Be sure all your maneuvers remain solid and correct despite the increase in speed and pressure for

the one maneuver you picked in the point above. Just being able to increase your scoring ability on that one maneuver may put you in a higher position on the leader board than much of your competition. Don't fall into the trap of thinking, "Wow, we really nailed those spins, I feel great, I'm going to try do that with my circles right now!" One excellent maneuver may win the class if the rest of the pattern is simply ridden correctly.

Additonal Qualities

As I've mentioned, the judge is looking for an extra degree of difficulty to increase the marks for each maneuver. It's as though the judge is saying, "Okay, you did that correctly; now can you 'up' your game?"

Finesse   This means flair, smoothness, and softness. Take your circle, for example. Does your horse remain in a consistent frame while moving from large fast to small slow circles? Is it visually appealing or do you see missteps that draw your eye away from the bigger picture?

Cadence   There are rhythms in a reining pattern; if you close your eyes you should be able to hear the beat and notice the difference between large fast circles and small slow ones. You should hear a steady buildup during the rundown to the sliding stop and the consistent footfalls of the spin.

Quickness   This refers to the reaction of the horse to the rider's cues—especially during spins and rollbacks. Does he respond so quickly that you hardly see the rider's hand move when he asks for a rollback?

Confidence   Your horse should not only display a willing attitude, but he should look like he knows what he is doing. There should be no signs of intimidation and fear; he should look as though reining is his job and he's a professional.

Authority   The "authority" of maneuvers is apparent when the horse listens to the rider's cues to begin and finish a maneuver with no hesitation. It's not just starting a spin quickly and correctly, but doing so immediately with no doubt.

PENALTIES

As I mentioned at the beginning of the chapter, during the ride, you may incur penalties that are applied

How the Rider's Body Position Affects the Score

Remember that your body position will affect your score only when it is obviously out of position or uncoordinated and is impacting the horse's performance. Your body position is not judged on its own.

to your score in the final tally. Penalties are the biggest stumbling blocks for beginning riders and avoiding them in your run can be challenging.

Each year, the *NRHA Handbook* is updated and it is common for a few changes to occur in the sections regarding penalties. Make sure you stay informed of the changes before you show by reviewing the current *Handbook* at the start of your show season. Changes are always highlighted in the book for easy reference.

I've included a list of penalties in the Appendix, p. 129, and described a few of the most common here.

Common "Zero" Penalties

Regardless of a rider's experience in the show pen, penalties will occur. Even the most experienced competitors make mistakes and garner penalties.

Overspinning   The most common "zero" penalty is to overspin. The forces exerted on your body during a spin and the sight of the world spinning around you can cause you to lose count of how many times you have spun. Rookies tend to keep their head down when riding, making it hard to count spin revolutions by using a stationary object like the judge, or a cone or fence post.

If your spin starts rough—either your horse starts too fast, or doesn't start the spin properly—then you have a greater chance of overspinning, or even underspinning. By the time you have corrected him and got into the spin, you may not realize which revolution you are on.

Two Hands on Reins or "Two-Handing"   A common mistake is to accidentally put two hands on the reins. Some classes allow you to ride with two hands from start to finish, but other than Freestyle classes, you cannot move from one hand to two hands during a pattern. When training at home, just about every rookie

"Suddenly, Bob realized he may have overspun."

Rules of the Reins

Excess rein may be straightened at any place a horse is allowed to be completely stopped during a pattern. When using a romal, no fingers between the reins are allowed. The free hand may be used to hold the romal provided it is held at least 16" from the reining hand and in a relaxed position. Use of the free hand while holding the romal to alter the tension or length of the reins from the bridle to the reining hand is considered to be use of two hands, and a score of zero will be applied with the exception of any place a horse is allowed to be completely stopped during a pattern.
—NRHA Handbook, B.5

relies on that second hand to fix his or her horse's lead change, gain control over his head, or straighten him out during a rundown. If you rely on that second hand, you are setting yourself up to reach out and grasp the rein when you become nervous or lose confidence while showing. To prevent this, practice getting through tough spots at home using just one hand, knowing it will be your only option in the show pen.

Even if you do incur a "0" penalty, an NRHA judge is required to continue scoring your run. This provides you with useful feedback. Other associations, such as the AQHA, do not require this.

THE SCORE SHEET

As mentioned, all 11 NRHA reining patterns consist of seven or eight maneuvers (see chapter 11, p. 76). While the judge is watching your ride, he reports each maneuver score to his scribe, who notes it in the appropriate place on the score sheet (fig. 8.2). While each maneuver receives only one score, the number of penalties can be unlimited and they are written above the maneuver score, but still in the column where the penalty occurred. The penalties are then tabulated at the right hand side of the page, just to the left of the final score. At the top, you will see acronyms for the maneuvers to be performed. You can see exactly what you scored and where penalties occurred.

NRHA JUDGES SCORE CARD Judge \ _____
Event _____ Date _____ Class _____ Pattern 4
MANEUVER SCORES: -1½ Extremely Poor -1 Very Poor -½ Poor 0 Correct +½ Good +1 Very Good +1½ Excellent

MANEUVER DESCRIPTION: RC, RS, LC, LS, SB, LRB, RRB, SB

DRAW	EXH#		1	2	3	4	5	6	7	8	PENALTY TOTAL	SCORE
1	256	PENALTY		½			1				↓	
		SCORE	0	+½	+½	-½	0	+½	+½	+½	1½	70½
2	143	PENALTY				0					↓	
		SCORE	-½	0	-1	-½	0	+½	0	0	0	0
3	210	PENALTY		½		½					↓	
		SCORE	+½	+1½	+1	+1	0	+½	+1	+½	1	75
4	178	PENALTY									↓	
		SCORE										
5	120	PENALTY									↓	
		SCORE										

8.2 *The standard NRHA judge's score sheet is used at every reining competition. Acronyms for each maneuver are listed at the top:*
LC = *left circles*
RC = *right circles*
LS = *left spins*
RS = *right spins*
SB = *stop and back-up*
LRB = *left rollback*
RRB = *right rollback*

At NRHA-approved events, a photocopy of the score sheets must be available for review or if one isn't available, you must be allowed to look at the original. It is very important to study it after the class has been completed. Many people write down their maneuver scores and penalties for further discussion with their trainer or coach. If the show is being videotaped, review your run with your scores in hand to see how the judge assessed the maneuvers. (Many videographers allow you to review a run while the show is still on—others will mail you a tape, for a fee, after the show is over.)

JUDGES

To become a judge in the NRHA there are several requirements: horse experience, a good level of expertise, good character, and exemplary conduct as a member and exhibitor, if applicable—though show experience or prize money earned are not required.

After attending an NRHA Judges Applicant Seminar and passing the required knowledge test, an applicant is invited to attend an NRHA Judges School. Several are held each year throughout the world. Once the applicant has passed the school's tests, his name is submitted to the NRHA Board of Directors to be considered for judging privileges.

The candidate must be at least 25 years old and a current NRHA member in good standing for at least two consecutive years to be approved as a judge. Judges must submit to retesting every two years or whenever the NRHA Judges Committee requires.

NRHA Judges' Seminars and Videos

There are two resources that can be very useful to a reiner at any level of skill: NRHA Judges Seminars and *Judges Videos*.

The *NRHA Judges Videos* were created to help teach judges how to judge, but also to help exhibitors better understand the scoring system. Available in video or DVD format, these videos explain every aspect of judging, including the often confusing method of applying the degrees of difficulty in maneuver scores. There are visual examples of each maneuver at a range of competency level so you can see just what a -1½ spin looks like, and how amazing a + 1½ stop looks.

Who Judges the Judges?

The President of the NRHA appoints a Judges Committee Chairperson, who appoints the committee members. The committee administers tests, conducts seminars and, if necessary, reviews the judging at approved NRHA reining shows.

After watching the videos, you may want to consider signing up for an NRHA Judges Seminar, hosted by NRHA affiliate clubs all around the world. Designed for the individual starting out on the path to becoming an accredited judge, the seminars are taught by judges and give all participants the opportunity to take an introductory exam to qualify to attend an NRHA Judges School. Many people attending Judges Seminars have no intention of becoming a judge, they just want to improve their understanding of the scoring system—they are a great educational opportunity for beginning reiners.

Participants have the opportunity to ask a qualified judge any question such as how to assess degrees of "overspins"; spot dropped leads; identify early or late lead changes; aspects of freestyle reining; and much more.

The Judge in His Natural Environment

It isn't hard to spot a judge at a horse show. He (or she) is the person sitting in a chair in the arena staring at you unblinkingly (fig. 8.3). Or, after judging 16 hours of runs, the one with an I.V. drip for coffee hooked up to his arm!

Between runs, during lunch breaks, and before and after the show, judges and scribes often are sequestered in back rooms or secluded corners of the showgrounds. They are required to limit their contact with exhibitors, owners, and horses before and during a show.

There are a multitude of restrictions placed on judges including when he can and cannot judge a horse (for example, not one he has shown, owned, trained, or been a sales agent for in the 90 days preceding the show). Because judges may also be competitors, there are also restrictions on when a judge may judge another judge and when a judge may compete. You can see the *NRHA Handbook* for further information on rules and restrictions that apply to judges.

8.3   *The judge and scribe spend long, dusty hours in their chairs. They may take breaks between classes or when the arena is groomed between runs or classes.*

Judges are hired by the organizing show committee and are paid by the day and often charge for overtime. Their travel and hotel are paid for by the show committee.

Sometimes you hear criticism of a judge. Remember, there is only one winner in every class and many who feel they should have won. A judge does not get paid to make people happy—he gets paid to judge fairly to the best of his ability. He is human and may make mistakes.

Judges' Feedback

At large, NRHA shows, you will get very little "face time" with the judge. A judge may check your horse's bit and have one or two words for you, such as "Nice run," or "Good stops," or "Looks like you need to work on your speed control." Or, you may hear nothing at all. He is not required to provide feedback or comment on a run, and some judges do not like to interfere—that is territory for you and your trainer. His real feedback will be on the score sheets. (After a class is over, copies of the judge's sheets are posted in a common area for viewing.)

However, at smaller shows you may be able to get feedback from a judge. Keep in mind that these "schooling shows" often do not use accredited judges. He may be a trainer or a local horse person. Just as with any piece of advice, it can be taken or left. See chapter 16, p. 113, for further information on the evaluation of your reining run.

9 Reining Equitation

Reining is judged solely on how your horse performs the required maneuvers; you are not judged by your body position during the run. However, your job is to help him perform and the best way to accomplish that is to improve your equitation: your ability to ride. First, let's go over some basic principles.

THE BASIC PRINCIPLES OF TRAINING

A reining horse should be soft and supple and "give" to the rider wherever the rider asks. This means he "gives" to pressure, say, on the mouth, ribs, or neck when pressure is applied. A horse "gives" to the bit when you put pressure on it and he releases in the direction of the pressure, and to the leg when you apply leg pressure to his rib cage, and he moves away from your leg. "Giving" is basically "giving in" to pressure.

The ability to "give" to pressure can take a long time for a horse to learn, but once he gets it, you will be able to train him. There are several key body parts you are going to have to learn to control in your horse.

Jaw, Mouth, or Face   You will commonly hear someone say, "That horse doesn't want to 'give' in the face." This means that when the rider lifts up his hand and puts pressure on the horse's mouth with the bit, rather than "give" in to that pressure and move away

from it (bringing his head down or into his chest), the horse braces against it and resists. It could be because he has not learned how to "give," he is feeling pain and seeking an escape, or he is stubborn and resistance has become a form of rebellion.

Shoulders and Hindquarters   It is important that when you place your leg or spur on your horse's body that you are able to move his shoulders and hindquarters wherever you want. This should happen when at a standstill and while moving by putting pressure on the rib cage closer to the front end or shifting your leg back. This will help you when you ask for a lead change, for example, because that maneuver is simply the ability to move the shoulders and hindquarters into a new position, which causes the horse to change leads.

Rib Cage   This is an important, but overlooked area by many riders. Not only do you need to teach your horse to "give" in his rib cage and move sideways, you need to teach him to lift it up. A "rounded" spine is very important to the reining horse. When it is round and his neck is lowered, the horse is in an ideal frame for a sliding stop. However, if your horse cannot lift his rib cage and round his back, he will not perform the stop correctly. Try it yourself: Get on all fours and try to round your spine without lifting your rib cage vertically—not easy!

9.1   *The proper body position keeps you solid and balanced in the saddle.*

THE RIDER'S BODY POSITION

It is important to sit comfortably and naturally in the saddle. It's not like sitting in a chair where you walk over and simply sit down; when riding, you are part of a moving object. "Sitting" becomes more of an action word (fig. 9.1).

Once you have climbed on, relax and let your legs hang. Your feet should be in line with your hips, your hips in line with your shoulders and you should be looking ahead so your head lines up with your shoulders. Once you put your feet in the stirrups, you shouldn't have to force them forward or backward into any position.

Once you begin to move, notice that you move with the horse. Don't think of the horse carrying the saddle and carrying you, but think about the partnership of you riding your horse. Your legs help to drive him for-

ward, and your pelvis and lower back are relaxed and move freely with his motion.

A great way to develop good body position is by trotting. Trotting builds not only your stability and balance, but your horse's as well. You can sit at the jog or you can "post" by allowing the natural stride of the horse to push you out of the saddle and then allow yourself to settle back down. The trot is also a good gait for warming up your horse.

What is really important, whether you are walking, trotting, or loping is that you keep your head up. Your head actually weighs quite a bit and when you are looking down, it causes your shoulders to round and hunch. When this happens, the rest of your body is also put out of alignment, all the way down to your feet, and you become imbalanced, which interferes with your horse's momentum.

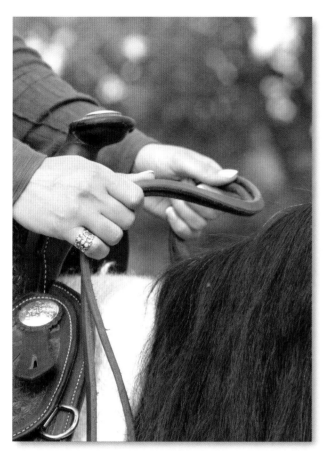

9.2 *It is common for riders to "bridge" the reins (as shown) when they ride with a snaffle and split reins, holding both the rein and the tail of the rein in their hands.*

HAND POSITION AND MOVEMENT

Your hands have a lot to do with how your horse performs. When their position is incorrect or your hands are moving too much, you may be cuing your horse indiscriminately, thus confusing him. The position of both hands depends on what type of bit and reins you use.

Snaffle Bit with Split Reins Ride with two hands and keep them low (just above the saddle horn), spaced 6 to 8 inches apart. Your arms should be relaxed and bent 90 degrees at the elbow. You can hold the reins with a rein entering your closed fist from the bottom of your hand next to your pinky finger, or between your ring and pinky finger. Either way, the rein comes out at the top of your fist, between your index finger and your thumb (fig. 9.2).

Mecate Reins with a Hackamore This combination also requires two-handed riding. The rein enters

Where Does This Arm Go?

When riding one-handed you might ask what you are supposed to do with your "other" hand. You can either keep your arm straight down at your side, or bent at the elbow and turned toward your body with your fist held at belt buckle level. Alternatively, you can keep this "free" hand 6 to 8 inches from your rein hand, shadowing the hand that is doing the guiding. Wherever it is, hold it in a relaxed and comfortable manner.

the hand at the pinky finger and comes out the top of your hand between your first finger and your thumb. All four fingers wrap around the rein. In this instance, there is a third "rein" that you can attach to either the saddle horn or tuck into your belt.

Shanked Bit with Split Reins Ride one-handed with this combination—most riders hold the reins in their left hand. Whichever you choose, the excess rein always falls on the same side as that hand (figs. 9.3 A–D). Hold the reins so that they come into your hand between your middle finger and your thumb with your index finger in between the two reins. (You are not allowed to have more than one finger between the reins.)

Shanked Bit with Romal Reins These reins are often made of leather or rawhide and form a "Y" with two single ends connecting to the bit and the tail (the two joined reins) of the "Y" held in your hand (figs. 9.4 A–D). Your rein hand is placed before the fork in the "Y" where the reins are separate, and your other hand must be a minimum of 16 inches down the length of the reins, holding the "tail." Your hands can be as close together as you'd like, but there must be 16 inches of rein between them.

The reins enter your guiding hand at the bottom of your fist and come up through the top with your fingers and thumb wrapped around them.

A common error when riding with romals is using your free hand to adjust the length of the rein while you are moving. This action results in a score of "0."

Whichever type of reins you use, you are permitted to adjust your rein length at any part of the pattern

9.3 A–D   *There are correct and incorrect ways to hold the reins one-handed. In A & B, the rider is holding the split reins correctly. In C, the rider is holding the reins incorrectly and attempting to guide the horse by using her middle finger to move one rein (here, the left). In D, the reins are again held incorrectly—the rider is gripping the outside rein (here, the left) in her fist and thereby making more contact with one rein than the other.*

9.4 A–D   *It can take some time to get used to riding with romal reins. There should be at least 16 inches of rein between your hands (A) and adjusting the length of the reins by using your free hand to pull them through your guiding hand is a common mistake (B). The romals should enter at the bottom of the guiding hand and exit out the top (C). Holding them incorrectly, with your fingers between the reins, for example, will result in a "zero" score (D).*

where you are legally allowed to be at a complete stop. For example, you can adjust your reins before and after your spins at center (because the patterns states that you can stand there), but not after you stop and before you rollback (because the actual maneuver is a stop and roll-back together). To make an adjustment, loosen your rein hand first and pull on the reins with your "tail" hand, shortening the rein length from the bit to your hands.

9.5 A & B   An experienced reining horse can be easily guided with one hand when the rein puts subtle pressure against his neck.

DIRECT VS. NECK REINING

"Guiding" is what reiners call steering their horse. If you recall, in chapter 1 you read the NRHA definition of a reining horse, and it stated that the horse must be "willingly guided" through his pattern (see p. 1). There are two ways to guide your horse: *neck reining* and *direct reining.*

Neck Reining   This type of guiding follows similar principles to direct reining (see right). You hold the reins in one hand—usually your left—and when you want to go left, you move this hand left. Steering occurs when the horse feels the rein pressure on his neck and moves away from it and in the direction you are requesting. When you hold the reins too tight, the horse may become confused with pressure on his neck and in his mouth at the same time (figs. 9.5 A & B).

The bit in your horse's mouth when you are neck reining should be a shanked bit (the "shanks" are the metal part of the mouthpiece that hang down, to which the reins are attached). I discussed this on p. 37.

Direct Reining   When riding two-handed in a snaffle, you move your left hand to the left when that is your chosen direction, and your right hand to the right if that's the direction you want to go. The guiding, in this case, comes through direct contact of the rein on the bit and on your horse's mouth (figs. 9.6. A & B).

USING LEGS AND SPURS PROPERLY

As with many disciplines of horseback riding, your legs are not there just to hold you on the horse. They provide direction and guidance for lateral, forward, and backward movement, as I will describe. When you have become advanced enough to be able to control your legs without gripping, you will be ready to wear spurs. Spurs are a training tool, and never to be used for punishment.

9.6 A & B   You can also guide a horse with two hands. This is direct reining—the horse responds to pressure on one side of the bit or the other.

When asking your horse to yield ("give") away from your leg pressure, first use your calf. You can flex your calf muscle by pulling your toes up and pushing your heel down. Then squeeze the leg against your horse's side, or if needed, you can also bump it against him softly.

When your horse does not respond, press the spur into the side of your horse. If he still does not respond, press the spur into his side and point your toe down and lift your heel up—all in one motion; this creates the action of rolling the rowel across your horse's hide, which is a bit more uncomfortable for him.

The next level is to bump your horse with your leg or spur. You should never kick your horse with your spur. The spur should always be used humanely and patiently; it should not be the first cue. Have patience when requesting he move from your leg before you begin to bump.

As soon as your horse moves, release your leg or spur immediately. This is his reward. If your horse kicks out at your spur, pins his ears, or threatens to bite your foot, then you should be more patient and use your spur less. Practice some basic groundwork, and ask him to consistently yield away from your finger or knuckle before getting back on. Stand at his shoulder (away from his hind legs) and watch his head for signs that he may bite you. (Refer to the many books and DVDs

Definition: Inside Rein

When you are loping to the right, for example, the right rein is the inside rein, and vice versa.

available on establishing basic respect for your space and your cues from the ground.)

During a reining run, you will receive a "no score" if you cause your horse to bleed with your spur. This most often happens accidentally when a rider's spur has become caught on a stirrup or cinch during a maneuver, or when the rider is seated in an unstable manner and grips with his spurs inappropriately.

Also, some horses have very sensitive skin that allows them to bleed quite easily. In such cases, a rider might choose to wrap electrician's tape around the spur's rowel (the part that moves on the spur) to dull it during a show.

9.7 A & B   *The inside leg and spur is kept off the horse during maneuvers like the spin (A). When pressure needs to be applied, use your leg first and then the spur, if necessary (B).*

10 *The Reining Maneuvers—Horse and Rider Mechanics*

When you first saw a reining horse perform a sliding stop, weren't you amazed by it? Such a feat: the slide, so much dirt, such a sudden, surprising move. To watch the Pros perform, it almost looks easy. As do many of the maneuvers. Before you try them out for yourself, let's review how they happen.

CIRCLES AND TRANSITIONS

Horse Mechanics

Circles seem so simple, don't they? But they are not. Circling is one of the most complex maneuvers because it includes loping in a cadenced fashion, lead changes, and speed transitions: three aspects that give novice riders a lot of trouble.

To perform a correct circle, your horse must be in a "frame," meaning he should hold his body in a position that allows his spine to be "round" (see p. 59); his shoulders should be elevated and his hind legs reaching far under his body with each stride. This frame should not change whether he is in a large fast, or small slow circle.

For your horse to speed up and lope faster, he has to engage his hind end and make every stride more powerful, not just quicker. If he increases speed only, it will look like a scramble and he may unintentionally slip out of lead behind, causing you to be given a penalty in competition.

Slowing down properly requires balance and skill. Your horse needs to stay in the correct frame: collected with his back "rounded" and shoulders elevated without balancing himself on the bit.

When traveling around a circle, your horse's body is bent in a slight arc. This means you can see just a little bit of his inside eye. When it comes time to ask for a lead change, he must be positioned straight with his shoulders elevated. Then, you ask him to move his hip in the opposite direction in preparation for the change.

Rider Mechanics

Theoretically, there is nothing different about riding a circle and a straight line. You should not change anything just because you are going left or right. The horse's stride will cause a slight shift in your body when loping: if he is on the left lead, your left leg will move forward slightly and vice versa when loping to the right.

Speed transitions do require a change in your body position. When going from a small slow circle to large fast one, you should lean your torso forward. This encourages your horse to speed up. Some riders even lean forward, lifting themselves several inches out

10.1 A & B   Note the difference in rider body position during large, fast (A) and small slow (B) circles. By leaning forward and lifting yourself out of the saddle in a large fast circle, you make it obvious to your horse when you settle back in the saddle that it is time to decrease speed.

"John Wayne Arms"

Have you ever watched those old John Wayne movies where the hero runs full throttle across the prairie? His arms are flapping to exaggerate the great speed and excitement of a chase.

You can see the same speed and excitement in the reining pen, except here the flapping arms aren't quite as entertaining. In fact, flapping arms detract from the overall appearance of your ride.

If you suffer from "John Wayne arms," work on developing a better seat—riding without stirrups or bareback can help.

of the saddle to encourage the increased speed and to make their next cue (from fast to slow) even more obvious to the horse (figs. 10.1 A & B).

When you are slowing down from a large fast, you should straighten your torso, sitting up and deeper into your "pockets." This is the area where the back pockets of your jeans are and you can sit "deeper in your pockets" by sitting straight up and tilting your pelvis so that the "pocket" area makes more contact with the saddle. This is a "slow down" cue that many reining horses are trained to heed.

THE RUNDOWN AND SLIDING STOP

Horse Mechanics

To perform a sliding stop, the horse has to coordinate many different muscle groups in almost every part of his body. Before each stop occurs in a pattern, there is the "rundown," which is performed at a lope in a straight line with steadily increasing speed. The sliding stop should be timed to occur at the peak of the horse's speed in the rundown.

Your horse must be correctly aligned before you begin to stop. This means that his head, neck, shoulders, and hips all face in the same direction. Technically, and according to the judge's score sheet, the sliding stop maneuver has already begun once you have started your rundown. If your horse is out of alignment, with either a hip or shoulder poking out, the stop will be crooked.

First, his back needs to be rounded. This is because his hind legs will need to drive underneath his body, which is difficult with a hollowed back. Second, his shoulders need to be elevated. When he elevates his shoulders correctly, it lowers his neck and assists in rounding his back. This creates a smooth, arced topline that allows the horse's hind legs to push underneath

10.2 A & B   Horses have different ways of stopping. As long as certain parameters are met, all styles are acceptable and correct. Some horses will stop with their neck low and their nose near the ground (A), while others keep their neck even with their withers and their nose chest-height (B).

his body. During the stop, the horse balances himself using his neck and shoulders. Sometimes you can hear spectators say, "He needs to break at the withers," when this doesn't happen.

Each horse has a unique type of stop. Some reach their head and neck as low as possible to balance, while others prefer to keep their neck up higher (figs. 10.2 A & B). The height of the neck is not nearly as important as the ability to elevate the shoulders. As long as the shoulders are elevated and your horse is "giving" in the shoulders or face, the stop will be correct.

Third, the motion of the feet is key to the sliding stop. As the hind legs push into the dirt the front legs "pedal" or walk, helping to keep the horse balanced and moving forward at a controlled pace.

Rider Mechanics

The rundown and sliding stop are combined maneuvers that can be the most difficult to master. This is because the initial action of the sliding stop happens quickly requiring precise timing on the part of the rider.

The rundown is a gradual increase in loping speed and you need to ask your horse to stop when he is at peak speed. Unlike a fast circle, you should not be tilting your body forward but sitting square in the saddle. Plan to say, "Whoa," when you are at a spot where

you know the ground is safe, or at a specific point in the pattern.

All trainers have devised techniques to help a beginner figure out the timing and coordination of his stops. When you think too much about the timing of when you say "Whoa," you will think yourself into a corner, worrying more about which foot is hitting the ground and when, than just learning by how your horse feels. And unfortunately, learning when to say "Whoa" is a matter of learning when it feels right.

The correct time to say "Whoa," is when the hind leg opposing the lead front leg is just leaving the ground. This allows the horse to continue to pick that foot up while bringing his other hind foot in with it and pushing (often called "planting") them both in the ground at the same time. Try not to overthink it; after stopping repeatedly you will learn to "feel" the correct moment.

Many trainers teach their two-year-old horses that "Whoa" means, in no uncertain terms, "stop." Additionally they teach non-verbal cues. A cue taught at the very beginning sticks in your horse's mind. Cues may include pushing your feet ahead or saying the word "Whoa" in one long drawn-out syllable or a staccato "Whoa" with a soft pull on the reins. Or, still other combinations.

Reiner Warwick Schiller, on working with your horse's body:

"In the stop, everything the rider's body does from the waist up is reflected in the horse's body from the cinch forward. Everything from the waist down is reflected in the horse's body from the front back. This explains why bracing for a 'jolting' stop actually creates that jolt as it is the rider's upper body leaning back that causes the horse's front feet to brace (shorten stride), thereby causing a harder impact at the beginning of the stop. If a rider's upper body is relaxed and doesn't change prior to the stop cue, the horse's front legs should be relaxed and they will be able to balance through the sliding stop and not brace. If a rider's legs are relaxed, the horse's hind end should be, too."

Beware "the Claw"

Some riders do not realize what they do with their free arm during their stops until they see pictures of themselves and are dismayed to see that they have "the claw." This happens when they hold their hand open and tense the arm. This problem can be solved by carrying two small stones in your "free" hand—you will not open your hand with something in it.

Learning the sliding stop can be a painful experience for many riders. When done incorrectly, your legs might hit the front of the saddle. Warwick Schiller is a trainer from New South Wales, Australia, who specializes in training Non Pros and rookies, and he shares his techniques for learning to cue for a sliding stop. He says there are several things to avoid.

"Don't think about the impending sudden halt because your body will brace in anticipation (see sidebar). Don't look at the spot where you are going to stop or look down at the ground because just the weight of your head movement telegraphs your intentions to the horse as it shifts your body position. And finally, don't try to make your horse stop by throwing your body into a bracing position and pulling on the reins.

It is important to not overthink your upcoming stop.

"What you should be thinking about is—paradoxically—not stopping at all. The ideal stopping position is the position you are in when you are running to a stop; don't change anything when you say 'Whoa,' and this will keep your body out of your horse's way."

There are three components to stopping properly:

1   Lower back: You need to keep your lower back relaxed. This is easier said than done when you have hurt yourself while stopping and your body has begun to subconsciously tense before a stop.

2   Thighs: Rather than thinking about your legs as "hinging" only forward and backward, think of them as swiveling, too. When you say, "Whoa," roll your thighs toward the outside, thus opening up your pelvis. This helps you absorb the initial impact of the stop and keeps your thighs from hitting the saddle swells as your body slides forward slightly.

3   Upper body: Your shoulders should be upright and your chest "proud" as you enter the stop. You may find that your shoulders roll forward at the stop; this is okay, but your torso should not lean forward.

Think of the sliding stop as energy moving from the horse, up your body and out through the top of

10.4 A & B How to stop (A) and how not to stop (B). In A, the rider is stopping correctly because she is sitting up and staying in the saddle seat as much as possible. Her legs are moving forward naturally with the horse. Note that the horse's body is forming a "C"-shaped curve from tail to ears. In B, the same rider is braced and stiff, which has popped her body out of the saddle. Note that her horse's back is almost concave from tail to ears.

your head. The energy is absorbed from the horse to your legs, to your hips, to your lower back, and up your spine. When you have any tension in your arms, shoulders, back, hips, or legs, that energy comes to a halt. When in your lower body, you will pop up out of the saddle; when in the upper body, your arms will flap upward or your torso will move suddenly forward. When you see a rider's shoulders hunch forward **at the**

How to "Hesitate"

Some reining patterns call for a "hesitation" between certain maneuvers, usually between a stop and a roll-back. Other patterns explicitly state that there should be *no* hesitation at all, so make sure you've read the pattern word for word (missing out on a required hesitation could be grounds for a "0" score).

The purpose of the hesitation is to demonstrate to the judge that your horse is completely within your control and awaiting your next command. It can be very obvious when a horse knows that after a stop there will be an immediate rollback, especially if he has consistently practiced the two maneuvers together or is completing the last of a set of the two maneuvers in the show pen. The horse that is not listening to his rider will anticipate and attempt to start the next maneuver without a cue. The horse that *is* listening will wait for a cue (fig. 10.5).

The most effective way to teach your horse to hesitate is to practice it yourself: keep your body still at the end of a maneuver; take a deep breath or two; and then calmly ask for the next maneuver. It's important that you practice the hesitation at home and in the show pen. It is not timed, so you can sit for several seconds.

10.5 A reining horse that is listening to his rider will settle after one maneuver and wait for his rider's cue, without fidgeting or anticipating.

stop, this is a sign that he is "cushioning" the stop or allowing that energy to roll his shoulders forward. As long as you do not hunch your shoulders prior to saying "Whoa'—as outlined in the points above—this is acceptable (figs. 10.4 A & B).

THE ROLLBACK

Horse Mechanics

After your horse has come to a stop, it is usually time for a rollback. To say that the rollback is simply a reverse in direction is overlooking the amazing physical feat that it is. The rollback requires your horse to elevate his shoulders and use his hind legs to balance while he moves his shoulders and rib cage in a 180-degree turn. His front feet continue to make contact with the ground during the turn.

Your horse does this maneuver very quickly. The center point of the rollback is the inside hock. He "turns over" this hock quickly and then uses his hind legs to launch into the lope (figs. 10.6 A–F).

Rider Mechanics

Basically a rollback is a half-spin and typically occurs after a sliding stop in reining patterns. A rollback turns in toward the fence or wall (or when it occurs in the middle of the arena, it is turned away from the judge) and ends with a lope departure on a new lead. You use the same leg to cue the turn and the departure. For example, let's say you have just loped on the left lead and run down to a stop. As soon as the stop is finished, use your left leg to cue the rollback and right lead departure. Keep your right leg off your horse's body to prevent giving confusing cues (see figs. 10.6 A–F for step-by-step direction).

You can allow your body to lean forward in the rollback because you must be in unison with your horse when he moves from the half-spin position of the rollback to loping. If you sit up too straight or allow yourself to get behind the momentum, he may leave you in the dust—literally. This is one of the reasons it is okay to allow your shoulders to "roll with the motion" of the stop as I mentioned earlier (see above).

SPINS

Horse Mechanics

The spin in slow motion is what many equestrians may describe as a "turn on the hindquarters." The inside hind pivot foot stays in place and the horse turns in a circle on the spot while the outside hind leg is used for balance.

The inside front legs reach to the inside of the spin and work with a pulling action to move the shoulders of the horse sideways, and the outside front foot crosses over the inside front to then push off so that the inside front can reach for another step.

Rider Mechanics

The second most popular how-to after the sliding stop is the spin. Both are intimidating maneuvers that make the uninitiated nervous about performing. In the first they fear flying over their horse's head, in the second they fear falling off or getting sick. Both are possibilities. Here are some tips to avoid feeling nauseated:

▶ Sit "deep in your pockets." If you don't know how, stick two small stones in the bottom of the back pockets of your jeans and sit back in the saddle so you can feel those stones.

▶ Look out *over* the tip of your horse's outside ear—do not focus on it.

▶ Don't look down. This makes you feel as if the entire world is moving.

▶ If you do get dizzy, walk out of the turn immediately and grab the horn to keep from falling off. Note that touching the saddle in any way will result in a 5-point penalty but fall off and you'll have "zeroed" (see p. 53)!

▶ When spinning, focus on one point and count each time you see that point. It might be a person, cone, or fence post. In the show pen, a popular choice is the judge. In your head you can count, "1 judge, 2 judge, 3 judge, whoa." This helps prevent you losing count of your spins.

10.6 A–F   *After coming to a full stop, the rider begins to cue the rollback and the horse shifts his weight to the back (A). The rider opens up her new inside leg, turns her head and begins to cue for the rollback with her hand (B). The rider stays with the horse, keeping her inside leg clear of the maneuver and looking where she wants to go (C). The outside leg continues to cue for the rollback while the inside leg keeps out of the horse's way (D). The horse begins the lead departure immediately as the rider is cuing for it, keeping her hand pointed in the direction she wants to go (E). Horse and rider move forward on the correct lead, in a straight line (F).*

10.7 *A rider needs to be in tune with his horse to perform a quick, correct rollback.*

10.8 *Spinning correctly is easier when you have a secure seat and good body position.*

Help from the Crowd

When a rider is spinning, you will often hear a holler from the crowd at about spin three-and-a-half. This is a friendly reminder to stop. However, do not rely on this to know when spin four is around the corner— one day your cheering section might not be watching closely enough.

Not surprisingly, balance and stability come into play when sitting correctly in a spin (fig. 10.8). Posture problems can be exacerbated during the spin thanks to the centrifugal forces exerted on your body. "Not sitting straight in the saddle, leaning into the spin, and twisting your body are common rider errors when spinning," says Schiller. On their own, these problems seem slight, but when combined with a spin, they can become more exaggerated until you fall off.

Another common problem is having a too short outside rein, something that most often occurs when spins immediate follow circles in a pattern, or when the rider has shortened his inside rein for the first set of spins and can't adjust for the following set. A horse's

body should be spinning in a slight "arc" position in the direction of the turn, and a short outside rein causes his body to be positioned the other way (figs. 10.9 A & B). Schiller says, "This results in the horse's head inverting and tipping his nose to the outside, for example, when you are spinning to the left and your horse's nose is pointing right because your right rein is shorter and making more contact with the bit. You may still be turning technically correct but you will end up with a lower maneuver score because the 'visual' is poor."

THE BACK-UP

Horse Mechanics

To back up smoothly and correctly, your horse's back (and spine) must be rounded and he must not brace against the reins. If he does, it will cause his neck to raise and his back to hollow, creating a very unpleasant picture. During the back-up, his hind legs reach and *pull*, while his front legs reach and *push*. This is— not surprisingly—the opposite of forward momentum. But it is not the reverse of the walk; a horse backing

10.9 A & B   Begin your spin by softly cuing to prevent overspinning—a quick start can cause the rider to miscount. Keep your inside leg "open" to give your horse a "door" to go through. Here a spin to the right (A), and the left (B). Notice the soft "arc" of the horse's body.

up moves his left hind and right front together and then his right hind and left front: diagonal pairs, like the trot, in reverse.

Rider Mechanics

The back-up is quite easy to ride, as long as you stay out of your horse's way. Sit straight in the saddle and don't not lean back or forward. Many riders feel that they need to lean back and pull on their horse, but this only causes the horse to resist and pull back.

Many reining horses are cued for the back-up in the following way: After you have said, "Whoa," and come to a complete stop, lift your rein hand slightly to make contact with the bit and your horse's mouth, push your feet forward toward your horse's shoulders, cluck softly, and bump the side of your feet lightly against the shoulders of the horse. As you become more finessed as a rider and as your horse begins to understand your cues, you will no longer need to use your feet.

Common Posture Problems

If you do not have a trainer who can watch out for the following problems, have a friend record your ride on video. Here are some of the most common faults in rider position:

- Leaning in during circles

- Leaning forward in rundowns

- Leaning to the inside during spins (dropping the shoulder to the inside)

- Improper leg position during stops

- Gripping with the legs or spurs during stops and spins

- Keeping the head down

- Rolling shoulders forward (other than *during* the stop motion or rollback)

11 *The 11 NRHA Patterns*

The NRHA has developed 11 patterns to showcase the talents of the reining horse (reprinted here by permission). At first glance, they look the same: six circles, eight spins, and three or four stops. However, the people who created them are all longtime horsemen and women who understand the horse's mind and developed patterns not just to test or "trick" him, but showcase his willingness and obedience to his rider.

You should not memorize every pattern. Keeping all the patterns in your brain is dangerous because long-term memory can fall victim to all sorts of "misremembering," such as which direction to spin first. Before each run, review the pattern that is posted outside the in-gate for the class. Do not rely on the one in the show program—you don't want a misprint to cause you to ride the wrong pattern!

PRACTICING PATTERNS

It can be tempting to practice a pattern at home to make sure that you are able to do it in the correct order. However, this is discouraged. When your horse performs the same order of maneuvers over and over, he begins to anticipate the upcoming moves before others are complete. For example, it won't be long before your horse is anticipating a lead change after your first three circles. But what happens when there is a stop instead of a lead change? Or, he might anticipate a rollback after every stop—then, when you ride a pattern with a back-up after the first stop, your horse might rollback unasked and you "zero." The job of a reining horse is not to guess which maneuver comes next; it's to be willing to do what he's asked and to accept being dictated to completely.

Vary your training routine. Don't practice every maneuver at every practice session—you can leave the spins out one day, and the stops the next. Choose one or two maneuvers to practice and trust that practicing the parts will make you better at the whole.

⟩ PATTERN 1

Run at speed to the far end of the arena past the end marker and do a left rollback—no hesitation.

Run to the opposite end of the arena past the end marker and do a right rollback—no hesitation.

Run past the center mark and do a sliding stop. Back up to the center of the arena or at least 10 feet. Hesitate.

Complete four spins to the right.

Complete four and one-quarter spins to the left so that horse is facing left wall or fence. Hesitate.

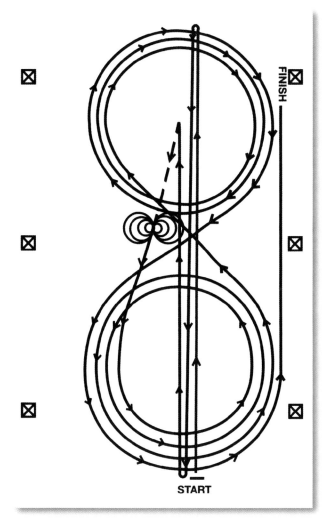

11.1 *Pattern 1*

**Reiner Chris Retterath,
on memorizing patterns:**

"When I have my reining pattern, I 'ride it in my mind' several times and make a summary of it on the back of a business card that I keep in my pocket. This way, I can double-check before I go in to the arena, whether the first spin is to the right or left. I break down the pattern into sections to memorize instead of individual maneuvers. For example, in Pattern 2 (see below), I think: 'Circles, then stops, then spins.' Then I break it down:

    Right, small, large, large
    Left, small, large, large
    Change
    Stop, stop, stop
    Back
    Right spins
    Left spins

"You don't have to remember all the details, because some become intuitive. For example, there are lead changes between the right and left circles because you know that you will have to change direction."

Beginning on the left lead, complete three circles to the left: the first circle large and fast; the second circle small and slow; the third circle large and fast. Change leads at the center of the arena.

Complete three circles to the right: the first circle large and fast; the second circle small and slow; the third circle large and fast. Change leads at the center of the arena.

Begin a large fast circle to the left but do not close this circle. Run straight up the right side of the arena past the center marker and do a sliding stop at least 20 feet from the wall or fence. Hesitate to demonstrate the completion of the pattern.

Rider must dismount and drop bridle to the designated judge.

◆ PATTERN 2

Begin at the center of the arena facing the left wall or fence.

Beginning on the right lead, complete three circles to the right: the first circle small and slow; the next two circles large and fast. Change leads at the center of the arena.

Complete three circles to the left: the first circle small and slow; the next two circles large and fast. Change leads at the center of the arena.

Continue around previous circle to the right. At the top of the circle, run down the middle to the far end of the arena past the end marker and do a right rollback—no hesitation.

Run up the middle to the opposite end of the arena past the end marker and do a left rollback—no hesitation.

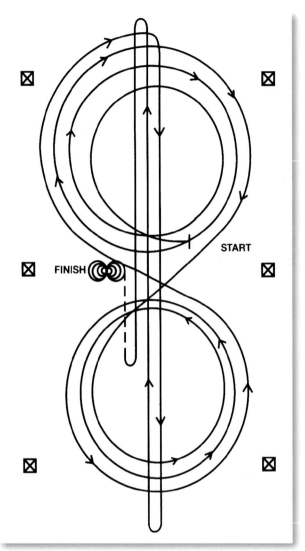

11.2 Pattern 2

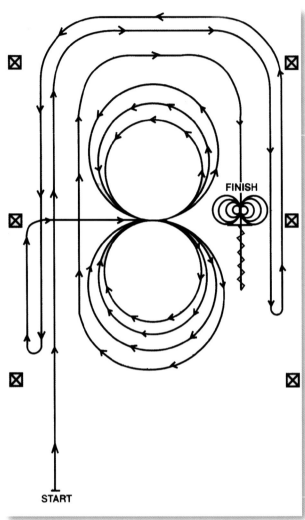

11.3 Pattern 3

Run past the center marker and do a sliding stop. Back up to the center of the arena or at least 10 feet. Hesitate.

Complete four spins to the right.

Complete four spins to the left. Hesitate to demonstrate the completion of the pattern.

Rider must dismount and drop bridle to the designated judge.

⏺ PATTERN 3

Beginning, and staying at least 20 feet from the walls or fence, lope straight up the left side of the arena, circle the top end of the arena, run straight down the opposite or right side of the arena past the center marker and do a left rollback—no hesitation.

Continue straight up the right side of the arena staying at least 20 feet from the wall or fence, circle back around the top of the arena, run straight down the left side of the arena past the center marker and do a right rollback—no hesitation.

Continue up the left side of the arena to the center marker. At the center marker, the horse should be on the right lead. Guide the horse to the center of the arena on the right lead and complete three circles to the right: the first two circles large and fast; the third circle small and slow. Change leads at the center of the arena.

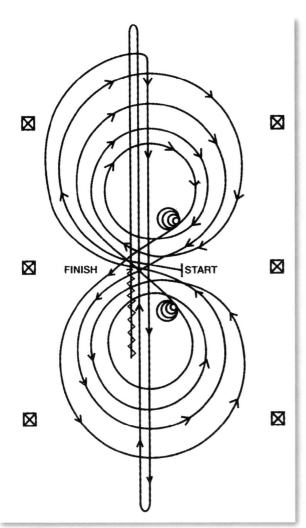

11.4   *Pattern 4*

Complete three circles to the left: the first two circles large and fast; the third circle small and slow. Change leads in the center of the arena.

Begin a large fast circle to the right but do not close this circle. Continue up the left side of the arena staying at least 20 feet from the walls or fence, circle the top of the arena, run straight down the opposite or right side of the arena past the center marker and do a sliding stop. Back up at least 10 feet. Hesitate.

Complete four spins to the right.

Complete four spins to the left. Hesitate to demonstrate completion of the pattern.

Rider must dismount and drop bridle to the designated judge.

◆ PATTERN 4

Begin at the center of the arena facing the left wall or fence.

Beginning on the right lead, complete three circles to the right: the first two circles large and fast; the third circle small and slow. Stop at the center of the arena.

Complete four spins to the right. Hesitate.

Beginning on the left lead, complete three circles to the left: the first two circles large and fast; the third circle small and slow. Stop at the center of the arena.

Complete four spins to the left. Hesitate.

Beginning on the right lead, run a large fast circle to the right, change leads at the center of the arena, run a large fast circle to the left, and change leads at the center of the arena.

Continue around previous circle to the right. At the top of the circle, run down the middle to the far end of the arena past the end marker and do a right rollback—no hesitation.

Run to the middle of the opposite end of the arena past the end marker and do a left rollback—no hesitation.

Run past the center marker and do a sliding stop. Back up to the center of the arena or at least 10 feet. Hesitate to demonstrate completion of the pattern.

Rider must dismount and drop bridle to the designated judge.

◆ PATTERN 5

Begin at the center of the arena facing the left wall or fence.

Beginning on the left lead, complete three circles to the left: the first two circles large and fast; the third circle small and slow. Stop at the center of the arena.

Complete four spins to the left. Hesitate.

Beginning on the right lead, complete three circles to the right: the first two circles large and fast the third circle small and slow. Stop at the center of the arena.

Complete four spins to the right. Hesitate.

Beginning on the left lead, run a large fast circle to the left, change leads at the center of the arena, run a large fast circle to the right, and change leads at the center of the arena.

Continue around previous circle to the left but do

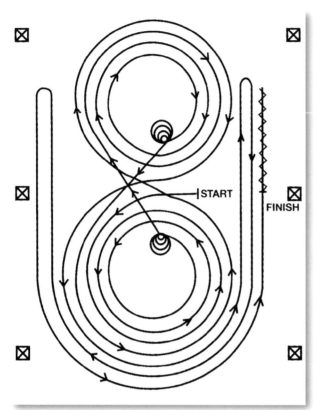

11.5 Pattern 5

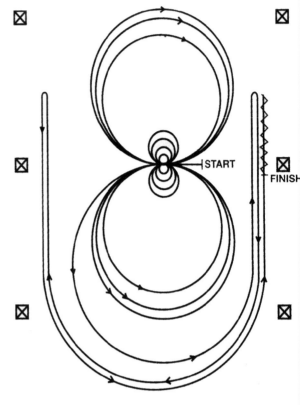

11.6 Pattern 6

not close this circle. Run up the right side of the arena past the center marker and do a right rollback at least 20 feet from the wall or fence—no hesitation.

Continue around previous circle but do not close this circle. Run up the left side of the arena past the center marker and do a left rollback at least 20 feet from the wall or fence—no hesitation.

Continue back around previous circle but do not close this circle. Run up the right side of the arena past the center marker and do a sliding stop at least 20 feet from the wall or fence. Back up at least 10 feet. Hesitate to demonstrate completion of the pattern.

Rider must dismount and drop bridle to the designated judge.

⦿ PATTERN 6

Begin at the center of the arena facing the left wall or fence.

Complete four spins to the right.

Complete four spins to the left. Hesitate.

Beginning on the left lead, complete three circles to the left: the first two circles large and fast; the third circle small and slow. Change leads at the center of the arena.

Complete three circles to the right: the first two circles large and fast; the third circle small and slow. Change leads at the center of the arena.

Begin a large fast circle to the left but do not close this circle. Run up the right side of the arena past the center marker and do a right rollback at least 20 feet from the wall or fence—no hesitation.

Continue back around previous circle but do not

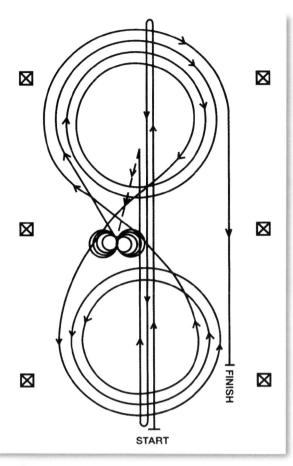

11.7   *Pattern 7*

close this circle. Run up the left side of the arena past the center marker and do a left rollback at least 20 feet from the wall or fence—no hesitation.

Continue back around previous circle but do not close this circle. Run up the right side of the arena past the center marker and do a sliding stop at least 20 feet from the wall or fence. Back up at least 10 feet. Hesitate to demonstrate the completion of the pattern.

Rider must dismount and drop bridle to the designated judge.

◆ PATTERN 7

Run at speed to the far end of the arena past the end marker and do a left rollback—no hesitation.

Run to the opposite end of the arena past the end marker and do a right rollback—no hesitation.

Run past the center marker and do a sliding stop. Back up to the center of the arena or at least 10 feet. Hesitate.

Complete four spins to the right.

Complete four and one-quarter spins to the left so that horse is facing left wall or fence. Hesitate.

Beginning on the right lead, complete three circles to the right: the first two circles large fast; the third circle small and slow. Change leads at the center of the arena.

Complete three circles to the left: the first two circles large fast; the third circle small and slow. Change leads at the center of the arena.

Begin a large fast circle to the right but do not close this circle. Run straight down the right side of the arena past the center marker and do a sliding stop at least 20 feet from the wall or fence. Hesitate to demonstrate completion of the pattern.

Rider must dismount and drop bridle to the designated judge.

◆ PATTERN 8

Begin at the center of the arena facing the left wall or fence.

Complete four spins to the left.

Complete four spins to the right.

Beginning on the right lead, complete three circles to the right: the first circle large and fast; the second circle small and slow; the third circle large and fast. Change leads at the center of the arena.

Complete three circles to the left: the first circle large and fast; the second circle small and slow; the third circle large and fast. Change leads at the center of the arena.

Begin a large fast circle to the right but do not close this circle. Run straight down the right side of the arena past the center marker and do a left rollback at least 20 feet from the wall or fence—no hesitation.

Continue back around the previous circle but do not close this circle. Run down the left side of the arena past the center marker and do a right rollback at least 20 feet from the wall or fence—no hesitation.

Continue back around the previous circle but do not close this circle. Run down the right side of the arena past the center marker and do a sliding stop at least 20

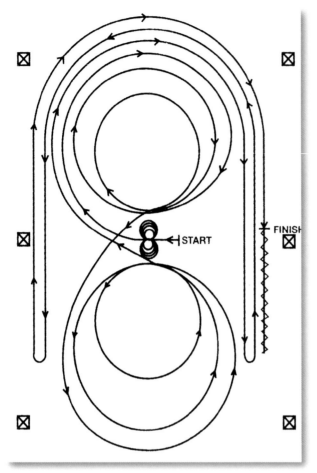

11.8   *Pattern 8*

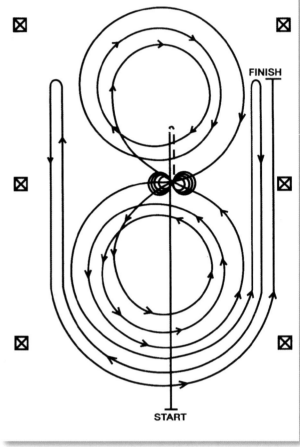

11.9   *Pattern 9*

feet from the wall or fence. Back up at least 10 feet. Hesitate to demonstrate completion of the pattern.

Rider must dismount and drop bridle to the designated judge.

⊛ PATTERN 9

Run past the center marker and do a sliding stop. Back up to the center of the arena or at least 10 feet. Hesitate.

Complete four spins to the right.

Complete four and one-quarter spins to the left so that horse is facing the left wall or fence. Hesitate.

Beginning on the left lead, complete three circles to the left. The first circle small and slow; the next two circles large and fast. Change leads at the center of the arena.

Complete three circles to the right: the first cir-

cle small and slow; the next two circles large and fast. Change leads at the center of the arena.

Begin a large fast circle to the left but do not close this circle. Run up the right side of the arena past the center marker and do a right rollback at least 20 feet from the wall or fence—no hesitation.

Continue back around the previous circle but do not close this circle. Run up the left side of the arena past the center marker and do a left rollback at least 20 feet from the wall or fence—no hesitation.

Continue back around previous circle but do not close this circle. Run up right side of the arena past the center marker and do a sliding stop at least 20 feet from the wall or fence. Hesitate to demonstrate completion of the pattern.

Rider must dismount and drop bridle to the designated judge.

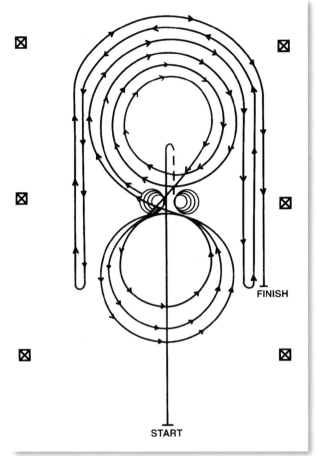

11.10   *Pattern 10*

11.11   *Pattern 11*

● PATTERN 10

Run past the center marker and do a sliding stop. Back up to the center of the arena or at least 10 feet. Hesitate.

Complete four spins to the right.

Complete four and one-quarter spins to the left so that horse is facing the left wall or fence. Hesitate.

Beginning on the right lead, complete three circles to the right: the first two circles large and fast; the third circle small and slow. Change leads at the center of the arena.

Complete three circles to the left: the first circle small and slow; the next two circles large and fast. Change leads at the center of the arena.

Begin a large fast circle to the right but do not close this circle. Run down the right side of the arena past the center marker and do a left rollback at least 20 feet from the wall or fence—no hesitation.

Continue back around the previous circle but do not close this circle. Run down the left side of the arena past the center marker and do a right rollback at least 20 feet from the wall or fence—no hesitation.

Continue back around previous circle but do not close this circle. Run down right side of the arena past the center marker and do a sliding stop at least 20 feet from the wall or fence. Hesitate to demonstrate completion of the pattern.

Rider must dismount and drop bridle to the designated judge.

● PATTERN 11

Horses may walk or trot to the center of the arena. Horses must walk or stop prior to starting the pattern. Begin at the center of the arena facing the left wall or fence.

Dropping the Bit

In each NRHA pattern, you are asked to remove the bit from your horse's mouth and show it to the judge. Depending on the show or class, there may be a pre- or post-check that may occur outside the arena before you enter or after your run before you exit. You must take the bridle off your horse (you can leave the reins around his neck for security) and let the judge see the bit you are using. This is done to ensure that the bit is legal (see figs. 6.7 A & B, p. 39) and that there is no twist in your curb chain. The judge may have a small tool with measured notches in it to measure the thickness of the bit. The bit check may be performed by the main judge, or by an additional judge in attendance for this purpose alone (see p. 95).

Because you are dropping the bridle without securing your horse (via tying), your horse needs to be okay with having the bit taken out of and put back in his mouth. He should also be comfortable standing still with just the reins around his neck—you do not want him getting away from you and putting on his own personal solo performance.

Beginning on the left lead, complete two circles to the left. Stop at the center of the arena. Hesitate.

Complete two spins to the left. Hesitate.

Beginning on the right lead, complete two circles to the right. Stop at the center of the arena. Hesitate.

Complete two spins to the right. Hesitate.

Beginning on the left lead, go around the end of the arena, run down the right side of the arena past center marker, stop and roll back right.

Continue down the end of the arena to run down the left side of the arena past the center marker. Stop. Back up.

Rider must dismount and drop bridle to the designated judge.

Once you have decided that you are ready to show you need to determine which shows and which classes are best suited for you and your horse.

NON PROFESSIONAL (NON PRO) VS. PROFESSIONAL (OPEN)

The NRHA separates classes into either "Non Pro" or Professional (Open). Non Pros may show in Open classes if they choose, but Open riders may not show in Non Pro classes. The definition of Professionals and Non Pros are clearly laid out in the *NRHA Handbook* (Show Rules and Regulations, Section B., 1. Non Pro Conditions).

Non Pro

Non Pros cannot have won more than $100,000 in Category 1, 2, and 6. Open reining competitions when they apply for their Non Pro card. A Non Pro cannot have "given lessons for remuneration and/or has not directly or indirectly shown, trained, or assisted in the training of any horse ridden astride for remuneration, regardless of discipline—this does not include prize money."

A Non Pro cannot have entry fees or expenses paid by anyone outside of "immediate family, or a corporation, partnership, or other business entity in which the Non Pro and/or a member of his/her immediate family

are the sole and only owner." However, expenses may be paid by someone else if the Non Pro is attending a demonstration, exhibition, is representing his country (National Affiliate) at an international competition, or is representing a college or university as an individual or part of a team.

Your Non Pro status is something that you should protect, taking care not to cross the line accidentally into Professional territory. If you do, the NRHA requires you wait a required number of years before you can re-qualify for Non Pro status.

Professional

A Professional is someone who gets paid to ride and train horses, or teach riding lessons. The NRHA has recognized one exception to the above: When the individual is certified as an instructor with the North American Riding for the Handicapped Association (NARHA) and teaches students either enrolled in an approved NARHA program (or taking riding lessons as prescribed by a medical doctor) then he or she is not considered a Professional and may apply for Non Pro status.

SO, WHICH ARE YOU?

The following examples illustrate the difference between

The NRHA's Definition of "Immediate Family"

"Husband, wife, parent, step-parent, child, step-child, brother, sister, half brother, half sister, aunt, uncle, niece, nephew, grandmother, grandfather, and in-laws of the same relation as stated above." —*NRHA Handbook* (Show Rules and Regulations, Section B., 2. Non Pro Conditions)

a Professional and a Non Professional. As you'll see the waters are murky!

Joe boards his horse at a training facility. He's a "seasoned Non Pro" and has won a few buckles and a few dollars at reining competitions. Tom is a new rider and often rides with Joe as he likes to see what Joe is doing and get feedback on his own riding. They usually meet up on Sunday mornings and Joe gives Tom some pointers. Afterward, Tom takes Joe for lunch and always pays the tab. Is Joe in jeopardy of losing his Non Pro status?

No; however, if Joe paid for a few lunches every once in a while, he would have receipts to prove he was receiving no tangible benefits from his relationship with Tom.

Tanya works two jobs to help pay for her showing habit. She recently started cleaning stalls at the stable where she keeps her horse in order to pay her board bill. The owner of the stable has also asked Tanya to lope his horse for him after she's finished her chores. He doesn't have time to ride very much and would like his horse kept in shape. He offers to let her ride his horse in an upcoming reining clinic with a big trainer in exchange for this extra, unpaid work. Will Tanya lose her Non Pro status?

Yes. Tanya is receiving remuneration in the form of "free" entry into the clinic.

Penny's horse needs more time and experience in the show pen and her friend Fred is a Non Pro who has the time. Fred plans to pay all the expenses and fees related to the horse, but the rules say he can't show the horse in a Non Pro class unless he owns it. So Penny

sells her horse for a dollar with an understanding that Fred will sell the horse back to her at the end of the year. They even sign the back of the horse's new registration papers (the ones that list Fred as the owner) that note the sale back to Penny so the papers are ready for her to file at the end of the show season. Is Fred in jeopardy of losing Non Pro status?

Yes. The practice of falsely selling a horse way under market value is forbidden under the NRHA's rules. The NRHA has the right to ask for proof that the fair market value actually exchanged hands. Also, there is a specified amount of time that must be observed (180 days) before Penny would be able to show a horse that she "bought back."

Donna volunteers to teach weekly riding lessons at her son's 4-H club. She isn't getting paid. She travels to all the regional events to coach the kids—she helps them remember their patterns and stay calm while giving them tips on riding. Could Donna lose her Non Pro status?

No. As long as Donna's instruction remains totally voluntary and she receives no remuneration of any kind.

Sally has a neighbor who wants to sell his horse. She agrees to ride the horse and get him into condition, without pay. The neighbor thinks it is a great deal—she gets the experience; he gets his horse in shape for free. After he sells his horse, he gives Sally a gift to show his appreciation. Could Sally lose her Non Pro status?

Maybe. This situation falls into a large "grey" area. Trying to prove that the gift is a result of riding the horse is almost impossible, unless they admitted it. What is the gift? Does the cost of the gift make a difference? What if it is just a very nice bouquet of flowers? What if it is a used horse trailer? If you find yourself walking in a grey area such as this, it's best to get out quickly.

Kelly, a student, wants to ride and show so badly she can taste it. She has limited funds, so she runs an ad in her local paper asking for sponsors to help her with expenses (gas money and hotels). This is often done when someone is a member of 4-H or Future Farmers of America. Does this jeopardize Kelly's Non Pro status?

Yes. Kelly's Non Pro status is in question because someone other than her immediate family is paying her expenses.

Ben goes to his trainer's place once a week for a lesson on his own horse. He pays cash for this lesson. The trainer also has Ben lope some other clients' horses to warm them up so he can get through his day more quickly. Will this jeopardize Ben's Non Pro status?

Maybe. It can definitely be argued that Ben is receiving intangible benefits by loping his trainer's horses. He could be jeopardizing his status because he has no "paper trail" and can't prove that he paid for the lessons; therefore, it might be viewed that he's receiving instruction (a benefit) for riding his trainer's clients' horses.

Ally goes out to her dad's arena where he is working on a client's horse. Her dad's cell phone rings and he needs to take the call. He asks Ally to get on and "finish up" for him before taking the horse back to the barn. Ally is young enough to still have a Youth Non Pro card. Could Ally lose her Non Pro status?

Yes. By "finishing up" a horse, Ally could be "training" him. Walking a horse (only!) to cool him out would possibly be okay, but to suggest that she "finish up" the last bit that day would also suggest that she participate in the training of a horse for which her family member is being paid—and she would indirectly benefit from that payment. To be safe, she should not ride any of the horses her father is training.

Robert, a Non Pro, buys a horse out of a trainer's barn. He takes the horse home but periodically takes him to the trainer for intense lesson sessions. Robert pays for the board while the horse is at the trainer's barn, but there are no lesson fees. Instead, during the course of his visit, he saddles and warms up horses for the trainer. Because Robert is away from home, he stays at the trainer's house. Is Robert in jeopardy of losing his Non Pro status?

Maybe. Robert appears to be working in exchange for his board. There is no money changing hands for lessons, so there is no proof that he is actually taking a lesson. By paying for his horse's stall, it could be argued that he is simply leasing a stall and riding for his own room and board; therefore, the lodging could be considered remuneration.

Tread Carefully!

Non Pro status is a privilege so it is important for Rookies and Non Pros to carefully adhere to the NRHA's rules in order to avoid the appearance of impropriety.

Showing Strategically

Start by showing at smaller, low-risk events that won't cause you to be "bumped out" of your league if you get lucky and win a couple of classes. Spend your first year only showing in classes that have very little "added money" in the class "pot" that is divided among participants that place in the class. This way you will not earn more than $200 in your first year and can qualify for the NRHA Rookie Class for as long as possible. This is the most competitive NRHA-sanctioned class for beginners and once you "earn out," you cannot go back. (Other classes allow you to go back if your earnings drop over a specific period—usually three years.)

Karen is 17, just out of high school and still showing in youth classes. Because she is small in stature, she accepted a job starting ponies at the local English barn. Is Karen in jeopardy of losing her Non Pro status?

Yes. Regardless of the discipline, Karen is accepting money for training a horse, and she's therefore violating the terms of her Non Pro status.

PREVIOUS EARNINGS

When deciding where to show, you need to know how much prize money you and/or your horse have already received. This is easy if *you've* never competed, but *your horse* may have earned money before he was owned by you. Note: Some competitions are separated into different categories and the money earned accrues in those categories as well as in the total earnings (see the sidebar on p. 89).

When you show in NRHA-approved classes, they have specific guidelines about "NRHA earning" or money won in NRHA-approved classes. And, some

Changed for the Better

In 2010, the NRHA offers a new show format for all skill levels. The four-tiered program will make it easier for reiners to start in a fun, educational, and family-oriented ladder of class and show formats. You can compete with others of the same skill level and there is an awards program to recognize rider achievements. It also includes reduced entry-level membership fees. Check the new NRHA rules pertaining to ownership restrictions and competitions licenses for these new classes.

Which Rulebook Should I Follow?

Open clubs holding non NRHA-approved classes will have their own rulebook that may include references to the *NRHA Handbook*.

NRHA-approved classes follow the *NRHA Handbook*.

International level events governed by the FEI follow the *NRHA Handbook*; however, many rules within are superseded by FEI Rules and Regulations.

Breed associations have their own rulebooks and while they often mirror NRHA rules, their book will trump the *NRHA Handbook*.

smaller open club shows (see p. 5) request competitors disclose lifetime reining earnings, which includes money earned at non-NRHA-approved classes. Member-based associations (like breed or reining associations, or local affiliates) can provide earnings reports if your horse has shown in their classes, and while some also award points (like the AQHA), they may have dual-approved events that award both dollars and points.

WHERE AND WHEN TO SHOW

In my introduction to reining in chapter 1, I discussed the various competitions and detailed the places where you can compete—starting with the easiest classes and ending with the world class events. In order, they are: open club; breed association; NRHA affiliate club; and finally FEI level. I also outlined the costs of showing in the reining world: buying a horse; transportation; memberships; and show expenses.

Depending on the level of your skill and that of your horse, you may enter the world of reining much as a child starting kindergarten. When you can ride but haven't quite mastered the art of the lead change, your first efforts should be at some schooling shows. These shows give you the best margin of error. This means, if you make a mistake, it will not cost you a great deal out-of-pocket because you will probably spend less than $100 overall—including your annual membership. So if you "zero"—it's not that expensive a mistake.

Schooling shows or lower level regional shows give you the opportunity to get some experience in the show pen. They are not NRHA-approved and are put on by open clubs to be used for practice as riders get ready for the show season. You can get over your nerves in a safe, fun environment rather than in an *uber*-competitive one. I will discuss these further in chapter 14 (see Dealing with Nerves, p. 103).

Once you have a few schooling shows under your belt buckle and are more comfortable running a full pattern in a show environment, you can work up to some regional or NRHA-approved shows over the summer. These may require further travel time and more expenses including hotel stays and overnight stabling (see p. 10).

CLASS LEVELS: BEGINNER

The smaller shows, like the schooling shows I referenced above, that are not approved by the NRHA or breed associations, are most often run by open clubs. They often have classes that the clubs name themselves (see examples below). Reporting your earnings (as described earlier) at these shows is on the honor system, but if you have purchased a horse that has already earned money in NRHA classes, you will have to know exactly what these earnings are before you sign up. Here are some sample open club classes:

"Green as Grass" May use a modified pattern that does not require a lead change. Also, competitors may be able to ride two-handed with a shanked bit, something not normally allowed in higher levels of

competition. This class is appropriate for the horse and rider with no earnings between them.

"Would've Won But Overspun" May follow one of the NRHA-approved patterns (see chapter 11) with money limits such as "less than $100 in rider earnings" but with no limits on horse's earnings, making it an ideal class for a beginner rider who has an experienced horse.

"Good as Gold" May follow one of the NRHA-approved patterns and have a money limit on how much the horse, alone, has earned. This is so a horse with $500 in earnings is not competing against the horse with $35,000, making it an ideal class for a rider starting out with an inexperienced horse.

It is okay to stay at the lower level for a couple of years, or longer, if that is where you feel comfortable. The patterns are generally all the same, no matter what the competition level. So if you are enjoying the competition, learning, and improving, then do not worry about advancing up the "ladder' to bigger competitions—unless you want to! (I talk about goal-setting on p. 107.)

CLASS LEVELS: AFFILIATES AND BREED ASSOCIATIONS

The next step after competing at open club shows are the NRHA-affiliate and breed association shows (see p. 5).

The NRHA affiliate is a regional association that has met specific conditions and paid a fee to the NRHA. The association may hold small unapproved "schooling shows" (that have little money awarded and are used for training purposes only), but will also hold larger shows comprised of mainly NRHA-approved classes. (For a complete list of affiliates, see the Appendix, p. 132).

The breed association show is run in a similar fashion. You will likely see reining classes that are approved by both the breed association and the NRHA, called "dual approved" classes. Because NRHA-approved classes are what you are most likely to compete in, regardless of the breed or affiliate, those are the ones I focus on here.

CLASS DEFINITIONS

Here are some of the class definitions that can apply to horse or rider. The more specific class definitions are

Tricky Terminology

Aged means that a reining class has some form of age restriction for the horse—either that he must be a specific age, within a range, or over a specific age.

Ancillary classes are NRHA-approved classes that occur at an "aged" event, but are not age restricted.

Concurrently run means that two classes are being held at the same time and in the same arena. If a rider qualifies for both classes then the score of his single run will count toward both.

Categories are what the NRHA separates classes into, and if a horse or rider earns money while showing in these categories it is earmarked as earned as such and may not count "against" him when qualifying for other classes. This is to ensure that horses can be successful in multiple areas—like breed shows, international competitions, or Youth classes—without quickly earning out of all other classes.

reviewed annually by the NRHA Board of Directors and changes are instituted to reflect the industry. Rather than list all current levels, which may be out of date quickly, I've chosen to list some general guidelines. Your best bet is to check the most current *NRHA Handbook* (available online) for specific qualifications.

Futurity A class restricted to three-year-old horses.

Maturity A class restricted to four-year-old horses.

Derby A class restricted to four-, five-, or six-year-old horses.

Open Open to any rider; there are no earnings, age, or breed restrictions.

ROOKIE AND NON PRO CLASSES

An NRHA Rookie can be either a Non Pro who is competing in the NRHA Rookie class, or a Professional rider who is competing in the NRHA Rookie Professional class, as you will see. This latter class was developed after the influx of professional riders found that their professional

NRHA Categories

Category 1 Used to determine World Champion and Top Ten awards; also used in NRHA-approved ancillary classes.

Category 2 Aged events such as Futurities, Derbies, and Maturities, where classes are restricted to certain age levels of either horse or rider.

Category 3 Youth classes and events.

Category 4 Classes restricted by the breeding of the horse such as Quarter Horse (AQHA) or Paint (APHA).

Category 5 Ancillary Gelding Incentive, Rookie, Prime Time Open, and Prime Time Rookie classes.

Category 6 Closed Aged Event classes, such as classes open only to progeny from a subscribed sire and dam program.

Category 7 Affiliate Championship Classes, which you must qualify to enter.

Category 8 National Governing Body (NGB) and Fédération Equestre Internationale (FEI) events, such as the World Equestrian Games or its qualifying events.

Category 9 Freestyle classes.

Youth Restrictions

Horses ridden by youths in NRHA competition must be owned by the riders or their immediate family or a corporation, partnership, or other business entity in which the youth and/or a member of his or her immediate family are the sole and only owner. Youth riders are not allowed to show stallions in Youth classes, but may show stallions in other classes (see also Youth Reining, p. 16).

status but inexperience in reining hampered their success, so they, too were given a Rookie-level class to compete in. For the purposes of this book, we are going to focus on Non Pro riders who make up the majority of the Rookie competitors.

Rookie Classes Open to Non Pro riders and without the restrictions of ownership for Non Pro classes as defined under NRHA Non Pro conditions (see p. 85 and the *NRHA Handbook*). Riders cannot have more than $200 in lifetime earnings in all NRHA Categories (except Youth) as of January 1 of the current year. Riders must not have more than 50 points in NRHA-sanctioned Youth classes (money is not paid in Youth classes or some would earn out of lower level classes too soon). Horses have no earnings restrictions and must be shown one-handed.

Prime Time Rookie Class Open to any rider who meets the NRHA's Non Pro definition and who is 50 years and older as of January 1 of the current year. *Concurrently run* (see sidebar, p. 89) with the NRHA Rookie class, and the rider must enter both.

Rookie Professional Class Open to any rider (except Non Pro, Youth, or Youth Non Pro members) who have less than $5,000 in lifetime NRHA earnings in all categories as of January 1 of the current year.

Non Pro Class Open to any rider who meets the NRHA's Non Pro definition.

Prime Time Non Pro Class Open to any rider who meets the NRHA's Non Pro definition and is 50 years and older as of January 1 of the current year.

Novice Horse Open Class Restricted to horses with less than $5,000 in lifetime Category 1 earnings (see sidebar) as of January 1 of the current year.

Novice Horse Non Pro Class Restricted to horses with less than $5,000 in lifetime Category 1 earnings as of January 1 of the current year and ridden by a Non Pro rider only.

Snaffle Bit or Hackamore Class Restricted to three-, four-, or five-year-old horses shown in a legal snaffle or hackamore. May be offered as an Age-Restricted, Open, or Non Pro class.

Youth 10 & Under Short Stirrup Class Open to youth riders 10 years old or under as of January 1 of the current year. Uses Pattern 11 (see p. 83). Riders may use a horse without the restrictions of ownership for Youth classes. Points are awarded instead of money.

Youth 13 & Under Class   Open to youth riders 13 years old or under as of January 1 of the current year.

Youth 14–18 Class   Open to youth riders 14 to 18 years old on January 1 of the current year.

Youth Rookie 18 & Under Class   Open to youth riders under 18 years old who have not earned more than 25 points as of January 1 of the current year. Riders may use a horse without the restrictions of ownership for Youth classes (see sidebar, p. 90).

Unrestricted Youth Class   Open to youth riders under 18 years of age as of January 1 of the current year. Riders may use a horse without the restrictions of ownership for Youth classes. However, if the rider does compete on a horse not owned by immediate family, the rider is not eligible to show any other horse in any Non Pro or Rookie class at the same show.

Breed Restricted Class   Dual approved class—by both the NRHA and breed organizations, such as the AQHA or APHA—which may include classes such as: Junior Reining, Senior Reining, All Age Reining, Amateur Reining, Youth Reining, Open Reining, Non Pro Reining.

Ancillary Gelding Incentive Class   A "class within a class" may be offered in conjunction with any ancillary class (see sidebar, p. 89) as long as the added money on the gelding incentive class is not greater than the corresponding ancillary class. Horse and rider must enter the ancillary class as well.

Closed Competitions   Classes not open to all riders but restricted to horses that meet criteria, such as being sired by a specific sire or dam or being subscribed to a specific sire and dam program.

What is the NRHA Rookie of the Year?

The "Rookie of the Year" competition occurs each November at the NRHA Futurity in Oklahoma City, Oklahoma. Rookies (not just beginning riders, but riders who compete in the NRHA Rookie class) from around North America qualify for the competition through circuit classes at their regional affiliate finals. Top-ranking riders from each region compete at the finals to determine the Rookie of the Year. It is very prestigious and often just getting to the finals signals an end to your rookie status. Once you have amassed more than $200 in NRHA earnings, you can no longer compete in this class.

A FLOOD OF FORMS

The journey to your first show actually begins weeks or even months before the actual event, when you fill out your entry forms and make sure that you have all the documentation and memberships that you require. Regardless of the level, carefully review the show's class requirements. For unapproved classes you will likely only need to have a membership for whichever organization is hosting the show, which can often be purchased at most shows or at the time of entry.

To show in the NRHA, you will need a *membership*, a *Non Pro card and declaration* (see sidebar, p. 92),

12.1 A–C   *The Lawson (A), Morrison (B), and Pewter (C) trophies are coveted awards at NRHA-approved events.*

April Clay, sport psychologist, on preparing ahead:

"First-timers should look at all the elements that can be taken care of ahead of time. Because they do not know what to expect, there can be a lot of anxiety generated by issues such as: How does the show work? What equipment do they need to bring? How does the judging work? How much time do things take (i.e., warm-up)? Alleviating some of these uncertainties can really help to calm the nerves. Apart from this, riders should have a clear and simple focus of what they want to accomplish."

Non Pro Declaration

To be granted Non Pro status, you must fill out a form whereby you state that you understand and have not violated any terms or conditions of being a Non Pro. You must agree to the "code of conduct and ethics" as follows:

I, the undersigned, agree to act with the utmost of integrity while participating in the sport of Reining and NRHA events. I understand that an NRHA Non Pro Card is a privilege and not a right, and that I may be required to submit my card for review of applicability at any time. Furthermore, I understand that so long as I hold a Non Pro card, it is my responsibility to be aware of and abide by the most current Non Pro Conditions set forth in the *NRHA Handbook*. By signing this agreement, I specifically agree to:

Understand and be bound by all by-laws and rules of the NRHA as set forth in the annual *NRHA Handbook*.

Abide by the show conditions set forth at all NRHA-approved shows.

Act with honesty and transparency when purchasing horses as well as competing at NRHA events.

Ensure the welfare of the reining horses I show and treat those horses humanely, and with dignity and compassion.

Refrain from violating the Non Pro Conditions as set forth in the annual *NRHA Handbook*.

Represent the sport of Reining and the NRHA by refraining from any action that discredits the sport, the association, or the association's membership.

Accept the decisions set forth by the NRHA Board of Directors.

and a *competition license* for your horse. While you can apply for NRHA membership and a Non Pro card at the horse show, a competition license must be obtained in advance. The good news is that only one license needs to be filled out for each horse and this is transferred to a new owner—just like breed registration papers. The application process involves submitting color photographs of your horse.

In addition, each individual show committee has its own forms to fill out. Here are some you commonly encounter:

Waiver This signed release acknowledges that you know riding is dangerous and that you won't sue the association should an accident occur on the showgrounds.

Breed Registration, Memberships, Non Pro Card, and Competition Licenses Photocopies of these will need to accompany your entry and it is a good idea to keep a binder in your trailer with about a dozen photocopies of each document. If your horse is a grade (not registered with any specific breed organization), you may need to have a letter signed by your veterinarian that states the horse's age.

Entry Form Each show package (sometimes called a show bill or a premier, which may be mailed to you or downloaded from a show's Web site) should have detailed information about each class and its rules: Whether the class is one-handed or two; earnings restrictions; amount of money added to the class; and if it is concurrently run with any other class. Review the rules very carefully to ensure that you do not enter the wrong class, as this is a common error for beginners. Choosing the classes should be a strategic choice that you make with your trainer.

Immediate Family Form If you are a Non Pro showing a horse owned by an immediate family member, you need to fill out a form that states *all* of your immediate family members, their NRHA membership numbers, and exactly what their relationships are to you. This form is kept on file with the NRHA.

13 Show Time

PLAN AHEAD

Developing a plan before your show will help you to combat stress-related outbursts. Not being able to find your good tail grooming brush may be a minor inconvenience at home, but it can seem like a life or death situation just before you enter the pen.

Keep your grooming bag, show clothes, and tack in good order, and separate from training gear. Have one bag for all your good pre-run supplies such as a polishing cloth to remove dust from your horse, a stiff brush to get dirt off your chaps, and a good wide comb to do one last run-through on your horse's mane and tail with a shine-enhancing spray. A bag with a shoulder strap that can be hung on your saddle horn, then on the nearest fence post, will help to keep the bag handy and out of the dirt.

Lay out your show clothes a day or two ahead of departure day. Choose which saddle pads you'll be showing in and match your show attire accordingly. If you live near a dry cleaner, have your Western shirts pressed and hung. (If already at the show, ask someone in the show office for the nearest dry cleaner. Some larger shows have mobile dry cleaners that stay for the duration of the event.)

The day before the show, pack your trailer, making a list of what you have or what you may need to buy. If you have everything packed but the horse, you will have a much more enjoyable morning when you leave.

PREPPING THE HORSE

One to two days before the show, clip your horse. He should already be accustomed to the buzz of the clippers—take care, as some horses seem to believe that the clippers are about to "eat" them! (For tips, see p. 32.) Other tasks for the day before are bathing (make sure that you allow your horse to fully dry before putting on blankets), and braiding the mane and tail. To prevent overnight manure stains, use a slinky (see p. 28) to cover the horse's neck from muzzle to withers.

SAFE TRAVELING

If you haul your own horse, before your first show of the year, have your trailer checked for mechanical and electrical soundness; your tires inflated to the manufacturer's recommended standards; and check that the ball and hitch are sound. Under-inflated tires reduce your gas mileage, result in uneven tire wear, and may cause a blow-out. Over-inflated tires make the ride rougher and also add to the risk of a blow-out.

Show Packing List

- Saddles (training and show)
- Saddle cover
- Saddle pads (training and show)
- Leg protection (splint, skid and bell boots, polo wraps)
- Shoe-pulling kit (pinchers, rasp, and hoof knife)
- Extra cinches
- Multiple bits (any bits your horse currently uses, as well as a snaffle)
- Extra chin or curb straps
- Extra set of reins
- Leather repair kit (leather string, knife, hole punch, Chicago screws)
- At least two buckets for every horse
- Stall fork and bucket or wheelbarrow for manure
- First aid kit for horse and human
- Feed: daily ration per horse x 1.5
- Regular minerals and supplements
- Mint drops or Kool-Aid® to mask water taste for finicky horses (Note: Test these agents at home first)
- Shampoo and conditioner
- Baby powder and Vaseline®
- Small sewing kit

Safety in Numbers

When possible, travel in a convoy with a group of other competitors so if someone breaks down there is help available.

Keep your truck in good shape as well. If you tell your mechanic the type of trailer you haul, the weight you pull, and the approximate number of miles you will travel, he may suggest vehicle improvements or modifications to make your truck more fuel efficient and safe. Have regular spring and fall maintenance inspections done on both truck and trailer.

Plan your route to minimize travel time. The longer your horse is in the trailer, the more fatigued his muscles get and the longer his recovery time will be. Map your route ahead of time by using an up-to-date road map or an online resource like MapQuest (www. mapquest.com). For the uber-technical, you can have a map downloaded directly to your BlackBerry™ or other handheld device, or use a GPS.

When you stop for fuel, food, or a bathroom break, check your horse. Don't just look at him, but reach inside the trailer and feel under his blanket or sheet. It is rare for a horse to be too cool during a trip, it is much more of a danger that he will get too warm.

Not all horses will drink when traveling, so do not be too concerned if you unload him and he turns away from the water bucket. Of course, don't unload halfway through a trip if your horse is likely to give you trouble when you ask him to climb back aboard.

KEY PLAYERS

First, I'll talk about the people you'll come in contact with at the showgrounds:

Show Secretary This overworked and (often) underpaid individual is responsible for accepting all entries; posting class draws, results, and judges' sheets; handling any issues that may arise at the show; and directing competitors where to take their complaints.

Show Manager Often a person in a position of power within the association hosting the show, he or she has been working throughout the months prior to the event, garnering sponsorships; scheduling judges; organizing volunteers; and getting entry forms designed and mailed. At the show, the manager also handles any immediate issues such as problems with the facilities or scheduling conflicts (fig. 13.1).

NRHA Representative This individual—a member of the NRHA—agrees to stay at the show grounds from the moment the show officially opens until it closes, or as long as the show office is open and the show is officially "on." He or she handles complaints, issues pertaining to NRHA rules, or unsportsmanlike conduct toward judges, show committee members, or other participants. The representative files a report with the NRHA after the show and includes information given to him by the judges, such as details of "no-scores"

13.1 *The show manager is involved in almost all aspects of the show.*

Announcer and Assistant The announcer is the voice of the show and responsible for relaying time-sensitive and important information as well as calling out the scores. He often follows a script to ensure that all the sponsors are recognized but the best announcers employ a casual, friendly, and inviting tone that engages the audience as well as keeping them informed.

GETTING SETTLED

Before you unload your horse, your first call is to visit the show's office to find out where your stall is located. If you pre-entered and pre-paid, you will also pick up the rest of your entry package, stable passes, program, and exhibitor numbers. Keep all this in a safe place.

Find out at the office if there is a designated area for parking your trailer. You may have parking outside the barn where you are stabled or access to a reserved a spot if you happen to have a camper or living quarters in your vehicle.

or what they believe are deviations by the show from NRHA standards.

Judge You won't have much contact with the judges other than when you briefly meet in the arena and show them your horse's bit (see p. 84). As per the rules, judges must have limited contact with exhibitors.

Gate Person The individual who manages the gate to the show pen checks that the correct competitor is entering the arena at the right time. Riders must enter quickly, especially in classes where longer patterns are being performed, or shows can quickly fall behind schedule. It is the gate person who keeps the entrances and exits organized.

Once you have found your stall, check it for any unsafe items (like protruding nails, broken boards or latches); adequate bedding; and a working waterer (if automatic waterers are installed). Once your horse is unloaded, watered, and eating comfortably in his stall, check him head to hoof for any bumps or bruises.

Get organized as soon as you can: keep your manure fork and wheelbarrow—clearly labeled with

The courage of reining judges is admirable. The scribes are a different story...

Time-Saving Tip

When you are bedding your stalls after you arrive at a show, clean out your trailer and re-bed it for the trip home. This saves time and energy at the end of the show when you are usually exhausted.

The Effect of a "Scratch"

Note: Even when other entries are scratched at the last minute, riders do not go earlier than their scheduled start times (see below) because judges must keep to the published break and lunch hours. And, of course, competitors must be assured that their classes won't start earlier than originally scheduled and posted.

Getting the Message

Keep a white board and dry-erase markers near your stall to facilitate communication between you, your barnmates, and your trainer.

your name—tucked somewhere out of the way or in the back of your trailer.

When you are stabled with your trainer, stall curtains may be set up. Often made of heavy canvas, these display the name of the training stable and its "colors," and are attached to each horse's stall with metal ties and clips. These curtains are also often put around the tack stall, thus converting it into a private room where riders can change clothes. Trainers also frequently set up a table with brochures and business cards advertising their services.

Included in your entry package will be the daily schedule and show program. Post the schedule on your stall, find your draw in each class, and highlight it. Note the names of the competitors around your draw time to help ensure you don't miss your run. Plan your warm-up times.

Highlight the start times of lunches and breaks, and make note of your classes. Although many shows print the order each rider starts, this list doesn't usually include "post entries" (those received after the deadline—rides that are always added to the very beginning of a class). You may be "Draw One" in a class, but when there are five post entries, you must wait through five riders, called "Draw minus Five," "Draw minus Four," and so on.

Also note on the draw when they will be dragging the pen between runs. This is when a tractor pulls a grooming implement around to smooth out the footing. Normally, the drags are spaced out as equally as possible. For example, in a larger class they may drag every eight riders, but in a smaller class they might drag every six.

By looking at the type of classes being held on a particular day, and noting which patterns are being run, you can have a good idea of how long a class will take. For example, if the class is a "*run-in*" *pattern* (see Pattern 1, p. 76), you can guesstimate that there will be about 15 riders per hour. If it is a "*walk-in*" *pattern* (see Pattern 2, p. 77), that number drops to about 12 per hour.

Classes that have a "bit check judge" (who makes sure each bit is legal after the run—see p. 84) will go more quickly. When there is no extra judge for this duty, the judge in the arena must get up and check each individual horse. Make sure to carry the program and order of the draw with you at all times so you can tell whether classes are running on time by listening to the announcer.

KEEPING YOUR HORSE HAPPY

It does not take a lot to make a show horse happy: plenty of water, feed, and rest. While warm-up and exercise routines are tailored to your individual horse, try to keep the sessions short and not taxing.

Check your horse's water constantly. Most show facilities use temporary stalls to house the horses and these often do not come with automatic waterers. If your horse is not used to a bucket of water hanging in his stall, he may inadvertently bump it or even poop in it during the night. Filling the water buckets should be the last duty each night and one of the first things you do in the morning when feeding. Engage in a little teamwork with your barnmates and fellow competitors: have everyone always check all the water buckets in your row of stalls.

13.3 *During your warm-ups, take time to relax and enjoy the horse show and your fellow competitors— you're in it for the fun, after all!*

Try to keep feeding schedules close to the times at home and made up of the same ingredients, including supplements and minerals. You may need to space out some smaller feedings of hay to combat boredom, especially if your horse is used to regular turnout. Horses are grazers and whether at home or at a show, benefit from smaller feedings throughout the day rather than just one big meal.

BUMPS IN THE ROAD

Take to heart the quote, "The only thing constant is change." Know that change is going to happen while you are at a horse show. Your horse might be tired or sore from the trip and when it comes time for your warm up, you might feel as if you are climbing on a whole different animal.

An older, more experienced show horse often comes with a little "show baggage" (residual stress from being shown so much) and may need a short reminder that he's on a training program. While this is no time to reinvent the wheel, reminding your horse who is in charge may be necessary. You can also ask your trainer to climb on and "fix him" a little bit prior to your run. This is often called a "tune up."

It's important that you don't get flustered and start changing your program the day of the show. Keep riding the way you have learned and keep everything as

Keeping It Clean

Pick the manure out of your horse's stall at each feeding. This not only makes the daily major cleanouts a lot less work, it cuts down the likelihood of having to deal with an unsightly manure stain on your horse.

calm and quiet as possible. A show should be, in a sense, a "vacation" for your horse. Nothing sours a horse more quickly than taking a trailer ride to a new place where the intensity of training is stepped up and the days are long and hard. Who wants to take part in that?

Instead, give your horse plenty of rest and relaxation coupled with short rides that are not as demanding as your at-home training sessions. Your horse will stay fresh and happy at the show and perform better because of it. Sure, he's there to do work, but it's more like arriving at a test after months of study rather than cramming for the test all in a weekend. Trust the work that you have done to get yourself to this point. If something feels as if it is going wrong, stop and reflect, rather than taking it out on your horse. (I cover warming up in detail in the next chapter–p. 99.)

Dealing with Extreme Weather

At some point in time you will experience unpleasant weather at a horse show. Showing in spring or fall in the north means you should bring a heavier blanket just in case your horse needs an extra layer at night, while summer in the south means you should be quite concerned about the heat.

Overheating is always a bigger worry than being a little too cold as it doesn't take more than a few extra degrees to go from warm to too hot. When you experience soaring temperatures, pay very close attention to your horse's water intake. You might also try using fans near his stall or misting your horse with water from the hose. A cool sponge bath can help keep him comfortable.

When the show is outdoors, most show committees do not stop in the middle of a class for rain. Everyone has an equal opportunity to get wet, and stopping for rain might mean that the pair that went right before the class was stopped had their ride in the worst of it, while the next horse got to wait for friendlier weather. However, when lightening, wind, or ice is a concern, the class is usually interrupted. Sometimes a sudden downpour means that there's no longer an outside warm-up pen. At times like this, a show will allow competitors to warm up in the main pen between classes, even though it adds hours to the show day.

When it is raining, try not to lead your horse anywhere; instead get on and ride to keep your saddle seat dry and your boots and chaps clean. Or, throw a waterproof sheet over the top of your horse—saddle and all—leaving your chaps slung across the saddle seat.

Take care of the rest of your appearance, too. Remember, if you have a felt hat, the water should run off but if you have a straw hat, you need to keep the water away so the straw does not swell and distort the hat's shape. There are plastic hat covers made specially for keeping hats dry (see more about hat care in chapter 6, p. 44).

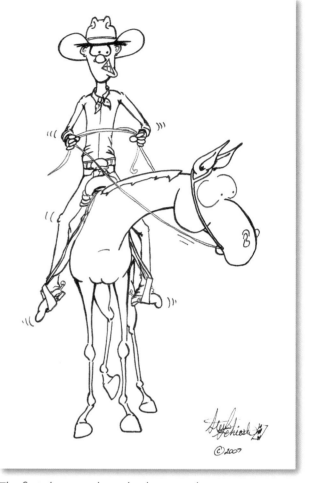

The first show can be a shock to your horse.

14 The Warm-Up: Horse and Rider

In this chapter, I first discuss the dos and don'ts of warming up your horse. Later, I dedicate some space to the stresses of preparing *yourself* for a show and offer some more general advice about mental pressure and how to deal with nervous tension.

THE WARM-UP PEN

It is easy to spot rookies stepping nervously into the warm-up pen at their first show. They are the ones holding their reins with white knuckles and shooting fervent glances in all directions to make sure they aren't running into anyone, while trying to avoid being run into.

The warm-up pen is most often a separate area away from the show pen that competitors can use to get their horse ready for their run. Sometimes the show arena itself is used between classes (such as during inclement weather—see p. 98). For the sake of clarity, I'll use the term "warm-up pen" to cover whichever place is designated.

Check with the show management about any restrictions as to who can ride in the warm-up pen and for how long. For example, there may be specific times for youth or rookie competitors. Quite commonly, the warm-up pen is left open overnight to allow everyone a chance to use it.

When you approach the warm-up pen, don't be intimidated by fast-moving horses, shouts of "Heads up!" and the apparent randomness of it all. Because as scary as it might seem, it is essential to warm up before you show. Remember, the warm-up pen is not the place to school or make drastic changes to any elements of your horse's maneuvers. That is what should have been done at home—there's nothing new you can teach your horse now. (If you do start to school or change the program, he'll learn not to like going to shows!) Keeping your horse moving, limbering up his muscles, and gaining exposure to the actual showing pen is paramount.

Trainer Roberta McCarty develops a warm-up routine at home with her Non Pros from the moment they start riding with her. She uses a guiding exercise at the jog and lope that helps them prepare their horse for the task ahead. "They turn in different directions, suppling their horse to make sure that he is following their commands," explains McCarty (fig. 14.1). "When we're at the horse show and we send 10 rookies out there to warm up for a class you can't watch every single one."

So the first thing McCarty tells her riders is to guide their horse around just as they would at home using the same techniques and skills they do in group lessons—

Warm-Up Pen Golden Rules

Be aware.

Be courteous.

Applying both consistently will assure your survival.

14.1 *To keep your horse focused, do some suppling exercises just before your start time.*

for example, avoid the traffic and don't run into anybody! The students are so familiar with this exercise that it is comforting at what can be a stressful time. They have confidence they can correct their horse and that he knows he has to listen.

McCarty puts it bluntly, "If we have riders who can't guide their horse and keep him at a reasonably slow pace without me watching, they shouldn't be at a show. They have to learn; that's the drill." By giving her riders a familiar exercise to work on independently, McCarty and her assistant have time to coach each rider in the warm-up before they show. The goal is for a rookie rider to gradually get to the point that his riding ability is good enough that he can warm up his horse on his own.

Warm-Up Pen Rules

There are always two circling areas being ridden in a warm-up pen and there is rhyme and reason to the direction of circle traffic: During reining patterns, horse and rider circle so they cross the middle of the arena facing the judges; therefore, when warming up in the show pen, always circle *toward* the chairs where they will be seated. Riders circling in the top half of the pen (located at the opposite end to the entry) circle to the right, and when in the bottom half they circle to the left. This way they maintain the same directional flow as they will ride when showing.

Every rider wants to practice each maneuver at least once, so general riding etiquette applies: do not ride too close to the horse in front of you; call out your direction if it is not clear to others; and move out of the traffic when coming to a stop (fig. 14.2). However, in the reining warm-up pen, there are additional rules that help you "survive":

▶ *"Heads up!"* is the most commonly heard call when warming up. In the most general sense, it is hard to see oncoming horses while you're staring at your saddle horn. It is your job to look out for those in front, while still knowing who is behind you: "shoulder-check" (look over your shoulder, both right and left) before stopping and do not back up without warning. Keep your eyes out for others shoulder-checking as it's likely they are about to stop or change direction.

▶ Riders loping circles have the right of way.

▶ Don't stop your horse in the center of the pen (often called "X"), but move to the inside of whichever circle you are on and then stop.

▶ If you want to *walk* or *trot*, stay to the outside along the fence and continue around the entire pen. But you must not *lope* around this perimeter.

▶ When spinning, go to the center of one of the two circles so you are not in the way of those circling.

▶ When it's time to cool down, walk the perimeter, or stand in the corners of the arena, out of the way.

▶ When socializing, do not walk two abreast around the edge. Again, stand in the corners to chat.

14.2 *Different maneuvers are performed simultaneously by many horse-and-rider teams in the warm-up pen. It's important to keep your eyes open.*

WARM-UP ROUTINE

Many rookies ride horses with show experience (see my discussion of the right rookie mount in chapter 4, p. 22). If you're one of them, ask the previous owner or trainer what sort of warm-up routine the horse is used to. If, on the other hand, the horse is new to showing, it is really a matter of trial and error. It may be best to start off by loping a lot of circles and getting him a little tired. Then, if you go into the show pen and find he is too tired, you can adjust the warm-up time to include fewer circles in the future. It is better to have a tired horse that you have to encourage to go faster than a horse so fresh he runs off with you or gets overexcited and unmanageable. Here's a sample warm-up that might be appropriate for most horses:

Climb aboard.

Walk around the arena both ways on a loose rein.

Begin suppling exercises, both ways.

Jog four circles each way on a loose rein.

Begin suppling exercises at the jog.

Jog entire arena and along diagonals with collection.

Begin loping.

Practice any maneuvers.

Performing some sliding stops is important when the warm-up is held in the arena where you'll be showing. It gives you the opportunity to test out the ground. Is the footing heavy, just right, rocky, or slick? Your

Fencing

The action called "fencing" often appears in the warm-up pen and is called such because it involves running your horse toward a fence or wall. To the uninitiated, fencing might seem a bit strange, but there is actually "training" going on. The rider asks his horse to lope and points him toward the fence or wall to teach him to gauge his own stop. You do not say "Whoa," instead, you let your horse stop when he feels comfortable. Fencing is often used with a horse that "anticipates" his "stops"; when a rider wants to test new footing (such as that in a new show arena) and how to stop in it; and when a trainer is trying to diagnose a student's errors like poor timing or incorrect body position.

When fencing in a rectangular arena you start at one end with your horse's hindquarters against the short-sided wall, and you lope in a straight line toward the far wall. When the arena is crowded there can be horses lined up at both short ends. As one horse leaves to begin his journey to the other end, his spot opens up for someone from the opposite end. Look from side to side when you lope off to be sure that others from your end don't have their sights set upon this open spot.

14.3 *Fencing—when you lope your horse straight toward the arena wall or fence—can be intimidating and requires you to trust your horse's ability to stop.*

Non Pro competitor, Chris Retterath, of Waterloo, Ontario, on warming up:

"To warm up my horse, without riding a pattern and without doing too much, I do some suppling exercises at the walk and then the trot; do some circles at the lope; and try some spins. I don't push; we're there to show in the pen, not in the warm-up. Before going in the pen I keep him busy, so his mind is on me. That may mean backing up; turning and walking ahead; or stopping and backing a few steps. I try to keep it low key, but he has to be listening."

Settling the Spook

If your horse shows signs of being spooky during your warm-up, you can handle it in one of two ways: Allow your horse to approach, nudge, and smell whatever is startling him and stay next to it until he's comfortable; or give him a job to do like spinning, counter-cantering, or loping in small circles. It is harder for him to worry about something scary when he is distracted by the job he's being asked to do.

horse may be used to a different type of ground at home. And, the show footing might be of poorer quality, especially when the arena is used for a variety of other events. However, ground that is not optimal for your horse may be fine for another and vice versa. That's one of the great leveling factors in reining: The ground is the same for all. You may have to make riding adjustments depending on how well matched your horse is to the ground. Will you have to ask for harder stops because the ground is heavier, or will you need to take care when circling because the base is very "slick" and therefore providing less resistance?

A "PAID" WARM-UP

Generally, show management hosts "paid" warm-ups during evenings at the show or even during days prior to the start of the event. When you feel that you or your horse might benefit from additional time or school-

ing in the show pen itself, consider purchasing one of these. They consist of five-minute blocks of time—normally costing around around $25—where you can be alone and mimic a real show environment. Most competitors even dress in show attire and arrange to have people sitting in the judge's and scribe's chairs so their horse gets really comfortable in the arena.

When you get to warm up in the show pen on your own, there are two main benefits. First, you can feel for yourself just how large (or small) that pen really is. Second, your horse can see that there aren't any large "boogey-monsters" living under the judge's and scribe's chairs, or hidden in the bleachers.

DEVELOP YOUR MENTAL SKILLS

One of the greatest reining challenges other than learning to perform the physical skills is developing the mental skills to compete. Cutting horse trainer and people coach Barbra Schulte teaches riders all over North America how to develop great mental skills. This is good news for those who get terribly nervous before a performance: Learning to calm down is a skill, not a God-given natural ability. Though some people are just calmer than others, *all* can learn to use their mind to enhance performance.

Schulte has written several coaching and riding books that focus on the Mentally Tough® Training program. In her book *Cutting, One Run at a Time* (Center for Equestrian Performance, 1999), Schulte explains the Ideal Performance State (IPS) as "a combination of many positive emotions (calm, confident, energized, focused, having fun, relaxed, and ready) happening simultaneously. You don't feel energized or just feel calm or just feel focused—you feel a combination of high, positive emotions all at once."

As Schulte explains, the techniques used to achieve IPS are skills you can learn. They include:

Create a vision. Visualize your reining run as a successful endeavor (see p. 104). Take it a step further and visualize your entire show career as a whole. Schulte suggests writing down your vision as well as looking to top performers for clues.

Determine where you are now. One issue that many riders confront is listening to a "self-defeating tape" running inside their head. This happens in the show pen when they make a mistake. They might have moved on to another maneuver, but inside they are still thinking, "Why did I say 'Whoa,' there? I missed my marker, I'm so stupid!" By taking note of negative feelings during training, at the show and in the show pen, you can learn to replace those thoughts with positive ones. As Schulte says, "You can never get rid of any negative feeling by *wanting* to get rid of it. You must identify the positive replacement and then train for it as you would train to perfect any other skill."

Develop good acting skills. Basically, this step could be called "Fake it 'til ya make it." By changing your body posture, facial expressions, breathing, and what comes out of your mouth, you can exude confidence. Schulte explains, "Most of us just show on the outside exactly the way we feel on the inside. From now on, instead of being at the mercy of your emotions, you can learn to control your emotions by controlling your body. When you train on the outside, you automatically train on the inside. By conditioning your body to 'act' like a calm, confident, successful rider, you take a giant step toward becoming that rider within." Maintain a calm exterior in front of the judge and don't make a big deal out of small mistakes that only you know about.

Train your mind. Schulte calls this step "mental conditioning" and it involves repeating positive messages, visualization, self-analysis, and acceptance of challenges. Your horse may throw a shoe, there may be a schedule change, or you could have a problem in the warm-up pen. "But when high-level competitors are faced with adversity, they will immediately search for solutions to problems or will place a problem aside if nothing can be done. They understand that difficulties are part of the game and they view them as challenges. Many world-class competitors who are trained in mental and emotional skills learn to welcome the tough times. It is as if they say, 'Give me more. I love this. I can handle it!' They do not dread difficulties but welcome them. They see that feeling challenged and rising to the occasion is what separates them from the rest. Adversity is a true test of your strengths and abilities."

Rituals. These are "habitual ways of thinking and acting" that get you ready to perform. "An example would be backing your horse, opening your shoulders, pulling your hat down and saying, 'I'm ready,'" explains Schulte in her book. "Rituals serve as anchors of pos-

itive emotion, which help prepare you to do your best. They are extremely personal. What works for you may not work for anyone else. What is important is that you figure out what does work for you and condition the ritual's association with feelings of calmness, confidence, and assertiveness. Be sure to use your ritual no matter how hectic things may get."

Recovery. This skill is especially helpful for reiners because it does not necessarily mean that you recover after a run, but that you recover between maneuvers in your pattern. "Take a deep breath and tell yourself to relax. You have just reduced your heart rate and brainwave activity, which will allow you to make good decisions..."

*Rookie Rule #876: Only **one** of you should be nervous.*

DEALING WITH NERVES

If you have never competed before, you do not know how you will feel during a performance. Some commonly seen reactions to nerves are nausea, increased heart rate and respiration, and perspiration.

Often riders refer to the intense "butterflies" they feel prior to a class. This feeling can be overwhelming, but not insurmountable. Roger Axtell, in his book *The Dos and Taboos of Public Speaking* (Wiley, 1992), writes that the key is not to get rid of the butterflies, but to get them "flying in formation."

While Axtel was actually writing about public speaking, a performance of horsemanship in front of people is not that much different—in both cases you have to demonstrate a certain level of competence. This is what causes apprehension. Instead of seeking to remove that feeling, make it work for you by focusing on creating positive energy and concentration—much like a baseball player does when preparing to swing the bat, or a dancer, waiting in the wings to take the stage.

Having a pre-ride ritual can help matters run more smoothly. After your warm-up, get a drink of water and allow your horse a quick drink, too. Touch up your horse's tail. Make sure splint boots, cinch, bridle, and any other equipment are correctly adjusted. Dust off your chaps. Review your pattern (see Visualization Techniques, below).

The Rider's Warm-Up

During your horse's warm-up, focus on the "right" feeling in your body and in your horse's body. Feel the nervousness and change it into excitement. Think positively about your upcoming pattern.

Do not let yourself get caught in a trap of just focusing on one maneuver. A common mistake is to lope circle after circle as "busy work" while waiting for your class. The rider who does this is often too nervous to *stop* riding; in fact, if she were to get off her horse, she would probably end up pacing back and forth.

Visualization Techniques

Visualization is a very effective technique, not only for memorizing your pattern just before you go in, but for gaining control over your emotions and helping those butterflies "fly in formation."

Take a moment in a quiet area. It is easiest when you can get someone to hold your horse while you sit on him. Close your eyes and imagine that you are running the pattern. Breathe deeply and evenly and visualize you are perfectly in tune with your horse at every move.

Do not imagine anything going wrong. The walk-in or the rundown is flawless; your horse speeds up exactly when you ask and slows down perfectly. Each stop is smooth and each spin, exact. If you have time, repeat this process. Resist the temptation to play the "what if" game where you imagine the good run gone bad.

Visualization isn't some cosmic wish for a good outcome. It is used by Olympic athletes as a mental rehearsal technique. By imagining and visualizing success, you create a feeling of success. When you enter the arena, it is as though you have already practiced several times. Your body will remember the movements and the maneuvers because you have done them before in your mind.

This technique also helps to keep you calm and relaxed because instead of sitting outside the show pen

Do not be dismayed by a tough pattern. Break it down into bite-size pieces to help you remember.

and worrying about your run, you have successfully performed it already in your mind.

Personal Space

Popular psychology states that there are two types of people in the world: introverts and extroverts. It is important to know which type you are. Basically, an extrovert recharges her energy levels by being around people, while an introvert recharges hers being on her own.

Knowing what you need will allow you to create the sort of pre-competition zone you need: one with friends to hold your hand or another with a buffer zone so you can process your emotions unfettered. When under the stress of showing, we develop coping patterns. Some riders need to talk about their coming ride, the weather, or ask their trainer questions. Others don't want anyone to talk to them and rebuff the friendly chatter of friends and family who are usually just trying to help.

Practice saying this, "I'm sorry, I don't mean to be rude, but I'm preparing for my class and can't talk right now." Your friends will understand, and those that don't understand, aren't your friends.

15 Chasing Perfection— One Run, One Show at a Time

In golf they call it a hole-in-one. Baseball players might call it hitting the sweet spot. For reiners, the ultimate goal is having a great run where your horse is in tune with your body and the connection between you is almost telepathic. You think "slow down" and he slows, you think "change" and he changes leads. This type of run is achievable, but it takes hard work, resilience, and a lot of "wet saddle blankets" to get there.

SHOW THE HORSE YOU HAVE

Time for a little tough love: There are better horses than your horse and there are better riders than you. But just as in any non-team competitive sport, the real competition isn't your fellow riders, it's you. To be successful, you must consistently improve upon your own scores and your own performances from previous shows.

If you spend too much time watching the rides of fellow participants, you may start to compare your horse and your riding style to theirs. This is a dangerous mindset. It's almost like the parent on the playground who wishes that her kid was just like "Johnny"—all the while failing to recognize her own child's unique strengths.

It not only affects how you view your horse at home, but how you ride in the show pen. Non Pro Jeanine Kern from Monroe, Washington, has learned this lesson the hard way. "Show the horse that shows up in the pen; don't take the entire pattern to try to convince your horse to become the horse *you want* in the show pen," she says. What Kern found herself doing was always trying to ride her horse for higher scores, and pushing her horse to do better when she went in the pen to perform. Realistically, this wasn't possible if he wasn't able to regularly do it at home in practice.

Focus on what your horse does right. Sure, you will need to spend time working on the weak areas, but what are the things that your horse does well on a consistent basis? There are some commonly overlooked strong suits of a good reining horse.

Strong Circles   A horse that performs strong circles can often be taken for granted by many rookie reiners. They are impressed by flashy stops and spins, thinking that points are won and lost depending on "wow factor" alone. But a strong circling horse—one that guides in a precise circle, has amazing speed control, is cadenced, and changes leads in an instant—is a solid horse to own. Horses that circle poorly—by leaning, not slowing or speeding up when asked, and fighting lead changes—will almost always garner their rider penalty points or cost them better maneuver scores.

Sound-Minded   If your horse doesn't get frazzled or try any funny business in the show pen, you have a real gem. There are many horses that ride perfectly fine at home and have amazing warm-ups but then fall apart under the pressure of the show. Or they behave poorly by dancing around at the center of the arena or refusing to stop.

Consistent Consistent performers are wonderful horses to own. It may take you all year to reach that coveted "70." Not to sound discouraging, but it has taken some riders more than a couple of years to break that mark. The biggest barrier in these cases is always penalty points. Too many times, novice riders overlook the horse that can consistently perform the maneuvers correctly, although slowly, instead spending their time trying to ride for a blazing score of 74 and racking up penalty points in the process. If your horse can do the basics, just ride him to the basics. Don't try to "out stop" the trainers or break sound barriers in your large, fast circles. Take the time to learn to ride in a consistent manner and build on your ability to achieve a score of 70.

High Energy vs. Lazy Horses

Is a high energy horse a "pro" or a "con"? It depends on how you look at him. A high energy horse needs a job to do. Oftentimes reining is a challenge for him because he expends a lot of energy trying to guess what is going to happen next rather than sitting back and wait for the command. This type of horse is prone to needing busy-work before, and during, his run. However, this horse teaches his rider to be focused completely on their relationship. There's no time to allow your mind to wander because this horse demands every bit of your concentration. Don't fight him, get used to thinking ahead, and keep him focused on the task at hand.

A lazy horse is the opposite of our friend above and is going to make you work for your ride. This horse often isn't stressed by show pen jitters because that would require more effort. Take advantage of his ability to come back down to a small slow easily and his willingness to "sit" quietly at center and wait for your next cue.

DAMAGE CONTROL

Understand and accept early on in your show career that everyone goes off pattern eventually. The best trainers in the world have gone off pattern, some at the most crucial times.

If you find yourself at a point in the pattern where you cannot remember your next step, pause and collect your thoughts. Think back to your visualizations before class, close your eyes for a moment and try to let your body remember which step comes next (see p. 104). Look around for clues. Unless you are the first rider in after the tractor has groomed the pen, you can see slide tracks in the ground so you will know where everyone else has been stopping. This might remind you where you are in the pattern. If this fails: guess. Think about what you have already done and what you might do next. Carry on and don't think about being off pattern, just about performing the maneuvers correctly.

When you know for sure that you have gone off pattern—perhaps you realize midway through a roll-back that you have gone the wrong way; you've lost track of the number of spins; or you are hearing that groan from the crowd that signals "Hey, you looked like you were going to win it until you did that"—you have a few options:

1 Finish the pattern.
2 Stop, dismount, and walk out.
3 Begin to school your horse.

All three are acceptable, but the best choice is the one that is best for your horse:

1 Finishing your pattern is most beneficial at shows where you know the judge will continue to mark your ride despite a zero score. Use the opportunity to get his or her feedback.

2 You sometimes see someone stop and leave in high profile competition: the rider, often a trainer, recognizes that it is now impossible for him to win, so he gets off and walks out, sparing the stress on his horse where there is nothing to be gained.

3 Schooling is one of the most popular choices. When you realize you have gone off pattern, you may hear your trainer shout, "School him!" This means you should train on a problem area, typically one that occurs in the show pen. You may

change from one-handed to two-handed or work on maneuvers your horse commonly "anticipates" in a competition setting.

Horses are very smart and can sometimes "cheat" the rider in the show pen, knowing that he won't be disciplined too much while there. There's nothing like throwing in five or six spins in one direction rather than four, or counter-cantering during your circles (that is holding your horse on the wrong lead in a circle to be sure he is listening to your cue to change) to keep him alert and paying attention to you. Or, if your horse is particularly nervous, break him down to a walk and remain low key to encourage his confidence and show him that the show pen is a low-stress environment. (I talk more about schooling through your run on p. 111.)

PLANNING AND GOAL-SETTING

As I mentioned in my discussion of trainers in chapter 2 (p. 12), at the beginning of each show season, sit down and determine your long- and short-term goals for the year. Knowing where you want to go can make it easier to determine how to get there.

Roberta McCarty discusses goal-setting early on in the client-trainer relationship. She's focused on helping her rookies have the most successful showing years that they can, and when she takes on a new reiner, she has specific advice before they even consider setting goals:

"My first advice is to stay as long as you can in the beginner classes and stay out of the classes where you might win money," she recommends. "You really want to spend a year or two down in the lower level classes and learn how to show a horse where the competition is not as tough."

Many of her beginning riders don't show in NRHA-approved classes for the first year. While many new reiners think it's fun to go to a show and win some money, most do not yet understand the way that money is tiered in the sport of reining. Once you've earned out of an NRHA Rookie class, you can't requalify (see p. 85).

"I don't even allow most of my 'Green as Grass' riders to show in the NRHA Rookie class because they may

Sample Short-Term Goals (First Year)

Consistently maintain penalty-free runs.

Learn to fence without closing your eyes.

Learn to feel lead changes without looking down to check and know when you are cross-firing (cross-cantering).

Have fun and make new friends*.

* This is an important goal!

Sample Long-Term Goals (Second Year)

Remain penalty-free.

Work toward riding consistent "zero" maneuvers.

Qualify for an affiliate year-end award.

Mark a 70!

Sample Long-Term Goals (within Five Years)

Have a consistent baseline score of 70 with the ability to "plus" maneuvers depending on your horse's ability.

Qualify each year for the North American Affiliate Championships in Oklahoma City, Oklahoma.

Venture into the world of "aged" events: Futurities and Derbys!

get lucky, make some money, and earn out. You need to learn how to show a horse effectively and without pressure, and have fun and win some prizes in Green as Grass (and other non-NRHA-approved classes) before you enter an NRHA Rookie class. Doing so will help you build a solid foundation of show experience."

A Trainer On Your Back—How To Ride Pattern 9

Many riders wish they could have a "trainer on their back," telling them how to ride when they are in the show pen. Trainer Roberta McCarty gives us her take on how a rookie should ride Pattern 9, a pattern fraught with potential pitfalls for the beginning rider (for all the NRHA patterns, see chapter 11, p. 76). Let's take it point-by-point with McCarty:

DIRECTION: Run past the center marker and do a sliding stop. Back up to the center of the arena or at least 10 feet. Hesitate.

"The first thing to address is whether or not a rookie should begin the pattern running through the gate from outside the arena or if she should walk into the arena, stand her horse at the back and then begin the run. I gauge how the rider feels about running in versus walking in and the horse's attitude about run-in patterns. Some horses get very excited while others can handle it better.

"Since we stress control in reining, we need to determine if the rider will be able to control her horse in this portion. If the rider is nervous about running through the gate or if the gate is not dead center of the pen, I recommend he walk in, get set up to lope off, and begin his run to the middle. (An offset gate means that the rider would have to adjust the straightness of the run, not an ideal condition for a rookie.)

"With bolder, more experienced riders, I advise them to run in from outside as it tells the judge right away that you are aggressive and want to score some points. One issue with walking in and setting up is that most of the time I find that rookies do not begin to build the speed early enough for the stop because it comes up so quickly: just past the center cone. Then because they are not accelerating the horse right up to the point of the stop, they miss the stop (meaning the horse doesn't stop) or execute a poor one. It's imperative, even in a bigger show pen that if you depart from the fence from a standstill, you must begin to build speed pretty quickly.

"Where to stop is determined by how well your horse can back up. If he's a good backer then 'going longer' (past the center cone several strides) is okay, but it becomes tricky if you have a 'sticky backer' who fights the back-up or isn't cadenced. In that case, the strategy would be to build speed quickly and hopefully not leave yourself a long back-up to the middle.

"Another strategy point to discuss prior to the class is which lead to run in on. I'm picky about that depending on the horse. Some horses lean to a side gate. If the gate is on your right and your horse is predisposed to lean toward it, you need

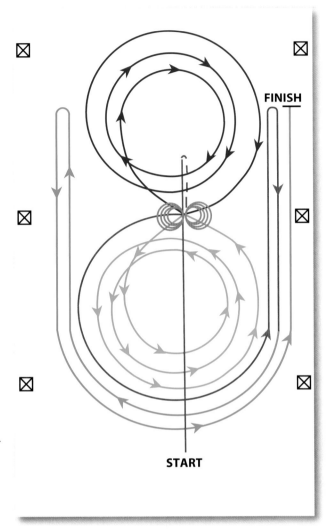

FINISH

START

to ride in on the left lead. If you have a horse that doesn't lean then choose the lead he stops better on. You need to know this prior to the show so you can practice at home."

DIRECTION: Complete four spins to the right. Complete four and one-quarter spins to the left so that horse is facing the left wall or fence. Hesitate.

"Here you should be calm while you *hesitate* and use slow cues with your hands and legs to start the turn. There should be absolutely no 'clucking' or 'kissing' to your horse until you count at least one revolution. This is because your horse may confuse that cue with a rollback. I don't let rookies practice rollbacks right before entering the show pen to show Patterns 9 or 10 because your odds of getting a rollback instead of a spin will increase considerably! Before the left spins the rider should again hesitate and use slow hands and legs to cue."

DIRECTION: Beginning on the left lead, complete three circles to the left. The first circle small and slow; the next two circles large and fast. Change leads at the center of the arena.

"After the left spins you have another hesitation. Take a big breath and think ahead: 'left lead, slow.' Move your hand slowly for the cue. Once you get past the middle (X) after one circle, begin to accelerate to the 'show fast' speed that you've practiced at home. I call this 'show fast' because it is important that this is no faster than the pace that you have trained for at home. Many riders show their horse faster than they practice at home—I like them to do the opposite so they are sure to keep control.

"When you travel through the middle (X) on your first large fast circle, you should not shift around at all in your seat, continue looking left and do not move your hand to the right as this may cue your horse to change direction or lead. Halfway around the second large fast circle, you need to begin thinking about the next maneuver: a lead change to the small slow right circle. Here you are transitioning from a fast speed to a slow speed and you are changing leads. It can be intimidating.

"This will make it easier: As you slow down when you come off the side fence or wall and are headed to the middle (X), the horse starts to decelerate and collect his gait. You are also starting to sit back and lift your hand to make contact with the bit, so the horse knows something is up. When you get to the middle, lift your hand, cue the lead with the correct leg, cluck or kiss to your horse, and move your rein over to the right. Your horse will change leads."

DIRECTION: Complete three circles to the right: the first circle small and slow; the next two circles large and fast. Change leads at the center of the arena.

"During your small slow right circle, remember to not make any sudden moves with legs, hands, or body through the middle (X) or your horse will anticipate another lead change, which we don't want. Then you have the two large fast circles, which you will ride the same as the other direction. This time, do not slow down before your lead change, but change in the same manner: keep riding and at the middle, lift the hand, change legs, move your hand left, and change leads.

"Now we want to gather the horse a little bit. Of course it depends whether the horse was excited through the lead change (as some horses tend to be) or laid back, but I gen-

erally tell riders that now is the time in the pattern to focus on getting or regaining control because things are about to speed up."

DIRECTION: Begin a large fast circle to the left but do not close this circle. Run up the right side of the arena past the center marker and do a right rollback at least 20 feet from the wall or fence—no hesitation.

"I teach my riders how to ride a 'rectangle' (not just circles) in the arena. I prefer that you have control over your horse and ride him in a straight line where it says 'do not close the circle' rather than simply following the curve of the wall to begin your rundown because your line will not be straight and neither will your stop.

"This pattern says you must stop past the center marker but try very hard not to look at the marker. This will make the horse 'set-up' (that's when he hesitates in the rundown because he is expecting you to say, 'Whoa'). Perform the right rollback, just like you practiced at home (hopefully): Stop. Drop your hand (or 'release' pressure off the bit), and then pick up again and make contact to turn your horse to the right while cuing with your left calf, clucking and actively riding your horse out of the rollback (as opposed to sitting still).

"We teach our riders to be aggressive out of the rollback because it helps to avoid trot steps (which incur penalties). If, after the rollback, the horse is going too fast, pick up your hand and make contact with the bit and slow him down before you come to the corner. If you have come out of the rollback on the wrong lead, change leads before you begin the turn around the end of the arena."

DIRECTION: Continue back around the previous circle but do not close this circle. Run up the left side of the arena past the center marker and do a left rollback at least 20 feet from the wall or fence—no hesitation. Continue back around the previous circle but do not close this circle. Run up right side of the arena past the center marker and do a sliding stop at least 20 feet from the wall or fence. Hesitate to demonstrate completion of the pattern.

"The previous instructions are repeated on the left side. Except on the last rundown and stop: Here, keep saying to yourself 'Don't back up!' as more than one rider has backed up and 'zeroed' for going off pattern."

California trainer Mario Boisjoli employs goal-setting with his beginners so that they can determine when they are making progress. He sets ongoing goals that riders meet with each run as opposed to simply achieving one time. "We try to make the goals believable and achievable for the rider; I don't want them to be discouraged by setting goals they could not possibly reach," explains Boisjoli. "The first is usually to stay on pattern, then later to have a run with no penalties. Once they can consistently achieve those first two goals, they're still marking probably about a 68. Then we can set a goal to try mark a 70."

Longer term goals may be set based on a particular achievement. There are many regional show associations across North America that have year-end awards and titles. Find out the associations in your area and which circuits you might want to compete in to win buckles and year end titles.

After discussing your short- and long-term goals with your trainer, you will both be aware of what needs to be done and what kind of commitment you are both willing to make. Your trainer will know to keep an eye out for horses for you and you can discuss your progress during lessons or during private meetings throughout the year. With your trainer's help, map out a course of action:

► How many times a week do I need to ride to achieve these results?

► How much money do I need to save for competition?

► How much money do I need to save for horse purchases when I need to upgrade?

► When will I be ready to upgrade my horse? How will I know?

By having goals and knowing what you need to do to achieve them, you will be better equipped to overcome rough spots during your show season. One bad run or one silly mistake won't leave you feeling as if you are completely off course and headed for disaster. To have the best runs that you can, you need to look at each run as a part of the bigger picture.

WHEN TO REGROUP

Despite your best intentions, you may not have the best year. You may experience setbacks such as a sore horse or financial concerns that affect your show plans (like rising fuel costs). The key to making it through rough patches is to have clear and open communication with those in your circle who are instrumental to your success.

If you have a trainer, he or she should know what page you are on in the plan you outlined at the beginning of the year. If you are harboring doubts about your current course, it's imperative you discuss them with your trainer and come to a solution that both of you can work with. Perhaps it's sitting out one or two shows or entering one less class at each show, or refining your goals depending on where you are in current competition standings.

Many close relationships can be forged at the barn. These relationships can be tested by competition, too close quarters at a show, and even envy. But if you are lucky enough to have a very supportive barnmate, make sure you tell him or her about your concerns. Getting a second opinion from someone who has your best interests at heart (your spouse, for example) can be invaluable.

There are three times you should take stock and regroup:

► When you no longer feel positive about your weekly lesson

► When you feel discouraged about your progress

► When you wake up worrying about reining horses

Roberta McCarty, while a serious competitor and trainer, reminds her riders regularly to enjoy the process. "When they get frustrated I remind them, 'You know what? It's not brain surgery—no one is going to die if you make a mistake. Enjoy the process, learn to show, keep the pressure off yourself, don't worry about the color of the ribbon. Just learn to show your horse.'"

SCHOOLING THROUGH YOUR CLASS

While you may take time out during the year to reevaluate your goals, when you have to take time to reevaluate during a run, things can happen at a pretty fast pace. When a run is going so wrong that there is just no use fighting it any more, you need to know when to regroup. Because there comes a time in every horse's life when he decides that he knows what he's doing and he knows where he's going and he'll be darned if he's going to listen to the rider on his back. Each horse will have his own way of telling his rider, "I don't want to listen to you." If this happens during a run it may manifest itself in several ways:

▶ Failing to slow down when asked during circling

▶ "Super-speed-rocket-booster" rundowns

▶ Tossing or shaking his head

▶ Refusing to change leads

▶ Leaning heavily to one direction during circles

▶ Kicking out or bucking

When your horse is behaving so badly that you cannot recover, it is time to "school" your horse. This means that you treat the remainder of the run as a training session, even if you have to deliberately "zero" by switching to two-handed steering, spinning extra revolutions, or "fencing" him rather than stopping in the appropriate place.

If your horse is displaying a bad attitude, defiance, or poor guidance in the show pen, then he is no longer "willingly guided and dictated to completely," and you need to take action to correct it. You hope this doesn't occur during the most important class of the show: you must decide if you want to try ride it out or if the class is insignificant enough to warrant schooling. Some trainers feel that there is no class outside of a finals run that is too important because if your horse gets away with it once, he will try again. Best to nip it in the bud.

When you have a trainer, discuss the possibility of schooling before you enter the show pen. A run may

be going along just fine but at any time the "wheels could fall off," and you should know what to do when you hear, "Go to two hands!" or "School him!" from the sidelines. This is usually how a trainer communicates to his Non Pro that enough is enough and it's time to school.

While Cory Hutchings prefers to school a beginner's horse himself, he views the ability of a Non Pro to school his own horse as progression in his training. However, it isn't something you should do all the time. "When you go to show a horse, you are just going to put your hand down and show," he says. "Normally, if your horse is making a mistake or two you aren't going to do a whole lot about it. You are there to show him." It's almost like pretending that the small mistakes aren't occurring because they might be mistakes that the judge doesn't even see, like a small behavioral problem or a lead change that isn't as smooth as you know your horse is capable. When you try to correct it in the show pen, the judge may realize that things aren't going as well as he thought. It's the "smile and nod" version of showing. But if Hutchings is entering a show pen with the intention of schooling, then it's a different story. "When you school a horse you let him make the mistake and then correct him. You surprise him by correcting behavior that he might have gotten away with."

Hutchings believes that not everything can be corrected by switching to two-handed riding to solve the problem. After all, the horse knows when something drastic has changed in the way you are riding, and you've then reinforced to him that he is no longer in "show mode" and now in "training mode."

"For example if the horse is leaning in on a circle, I'll let him, but then steer it out," he explains. "Something you wouldn't necessarily do if you were showing. If he's running off I'd let the horse go and then draw him down into the ground (pull him to a stop) to correct him. If he shuts down early (decelerates during a rundown and anticipates the stop) then I'd let him shut down but then push him fast to the fence. Let him make a mistake and then correct it, that's the basic premise of schooling your horse."

The object, says Hutchings, is to teach your horse what he's doing wrong, not to protect him from it during your run. "Sometimes you can feel that your horse is going to make a mistake, but if you protect that horse from making a mistake every time, he won't learn. I tell a lot of my Non Pros to go out and show their horse as if he's not going to slip up. If he does, fix it quickly and then go back to thinking that he's going to do fine again. Sometimes you have to trust your horse to perform."

FOCUSING DURING THE RUN

Surprisingly, it isn't that hard to focus during a reining run. That's part of the problem. A rider can be over-focused on every maneuver as it happens. To exacerbate things, it can seem that every person in the building is watching and critiquing your ride.

Several patterns call for a *hesitation*. This is to demonstrate that your horse is listening to you and willing to wait on your commands (see p. 71). This is also a good time to refocus. Sit still and take a deep breath in through your nose and out your mouth. This will help to keep your mind focused but relaxed. You can't over-focus and relax at the same time, just the way you can't clench your jaw while smiling nicely.

The most common reason that a rookie goes off pattern or loses focus during a run is a small mistake. And if you're over-focused then a small molehill mistake suddenly seems like a mountain. These can be as simple as delayed or late lead changes, a stumble, or a horse going too fast. If you have made mistakes in the run, especially if it was your mistake and not your horse's, it's important not to think negatively.

"A lot of people get real serious when they make a mistake and they get mad at themselves, even while they are still in the middle of showing, " says Roberta McCarty. "That's the worst thing you can do. If you get mad at yourself you are totally not thinking, and you are not conducting your horse (telling him what you want him to do) and you are not executing (performing). You just have to throw it off and go to the next maneuver, but that does take practice."

It's a philosophy that you have to wholeheartedly adopt in the show pen: nothing can change the maneuvers in the past. Focus only on having the best maneuver now and think about what is coming next.

McCarty believes that not watching other competitors actually exacerbates a poor run. "The rider goes in, has a mess, and is really mad at herself because she didn't perform. So she puts her horse away and leaves," explains McCarty. "You've learned absolutely nothing when you do that. It's very rare that your mistakes are worse or any different from anyone else's in the rookie classes. I really think beginners need to watch other people in their division. It doesn't really help to go watch the big name open riders show because that's not going to relate to your performance. But if you watch 60 rookies you are going to realize that they don't look any different from you."

16 Evaluating a Run

There are two ways to evaluate your run. The first is an objective evaluation in the form of a score sheet based on a judge's opinion, free from personal considerations or emotional perspectives. The second is more subjective—an evaluation based on how you have performed in the past, what you (and your trainer) feel you are capable of, and an assessment of where you need to improve.

INTERPRETING THE JUDGE'S SCORE SHEET

The judge's score sheets are taken from the scribe (after the judge has signed them) to the show office to have the math double-checked and calculated. Then photocopies are made and the sheets are posted in a public area. Your unique exhibitor and draw numbers will be listed and you can see the maneuver scores and penalty points you received. By going through the run maneuver by maneuver with the score sheet, you can get a better idea of the judge's opinion.

Keep in mind that while each judge should be judging to the exact same set of standards, you may encounter some differences simply because judges are human and cannot possibly be free from bias. Judges will say that they do not judge based on stylistic dif-

ferences, but the reality is that one judge may prefer a maneuver to be performed in a certain way.

If you "zeroed" and don't know why, the judge's score sheets will tell you exactly where the critical error occurred. If you are having a hard time figuring out what you did to incur a low score, copy your scores and penalties and go over them while you review your run on video. At many shows (especially NRHA-approved ones) there are videographers that tape each run as it occurs. These tapes are often used during video reviews, which can be requested by the judges when allowed (see sidebar, p. 114).

REVIEWING YOUR RUN

In the same way that many of us don't like to hear our voices on tape, some riders don't like to watch their run on video. "Is that me?" they ask. "Why is my arm moving like that in my stop?" Watching yourself ride is a great learning tool because you are experiencing the run as a spectator. By removing yourself from the physical experience, you will be able to see what worked well and what didn't. Plus, you can see if you remembered to apply what you'd practiced—for example, improving your body position and keeping your head up and looking forward.

The Judge and Video Reviews

According to the NRHA Rules for Judging (see pp. 53 and 129) "Judges may not confer on any penalty or maneuver score prior to submitting a score. If a major penalty (a penalty which results in a no score, a 0, or a 5-point penalty) is unclear, a judge will submit his/her score and ask that the score be held, pending a conference or review of the official video at the next drag or as soon as practical. Should the judges determine via conference or video replay that a penalty was incurred, it should be applied. If, however, no penalty occurred, the score will be announced as originally submitted. No judge shall be required to change his/her score following a conference or video replay. Each judge's decision is an individual call and based on individual decision from a conference or video replay. The use of video equipment by the judges is only permissible if the judge has reason to believe that all entries have been videotaped."

Show Diary

Keeping a catalog of your scores over the course of a season can provide invaluable data to show you where you are getting better and what you still need to improve. In the Appendix (p. 128) there is a sample competition diary that shows you how to record all aspects of your show season.

However, the real learning experience comes from reviewing the unsuccessful portions of your run. You can see mistakes like where your horse "set up" on you before your stop or where you accidentally spurred him when changing leads. Watch with a trainer or a knowledgeable friend who can help identify problem areas and make suggestions for future runs.

According to trainer Roberta McCarty, reviewing mistakes in a run is crucial, but so is planning for the next run so they don't happen again. "A beginner usually makes mistakes because his horse went faster than he thought he would or maybe spun faster and he lost count. But after recognizing where things went wrong,

16.1   *Reviewing your run on video is a great way to learn from your mistakes.*

you need to decide how you are going to try to improve in the future. If you don't, you are just wasting energy thinking about the past instead of the future."

"TRAINER SPEAK": A DICTIONARY

If you have ridden with a trainer for a long time, you may be able to translate his "catch phrases" into actionable tasks. However, when reviewing your runs and asking for direction, "trainer-speak" can really throw new riders for a loop. Here's a basic dictionary:

Bumping
"Bump on him." *Can be with hands or legs; it's not jerking or kicking, just moving them softly and repetitively against the horse.*

Came back to you like a puppy on a string
"If you sit down during those small slows, he'll come back to you like a puppy on a string." *You won't have to pull on him, he'll just slow down for you.*

Dialed in
"Your horse was really dialed in on that run!" *Your horse was really paying attention to your cues.*

Fractious
"He looks a little fractious this morning." *Your horse is unruly and likely to make trouble this morning.*

Keep riding

"C'mon! Keep riding, keep riding!" *Usually yelled from the fence during a run when it looks like the horse or rider is tiring and running out of steam. You may need to push your horse.*

Knock on his door

"Don't put up with that, knock on his door." *Used when you need to get after your horse, like in the spin when you have asked him to speed up and he hasn't.*

Lugging

"Don't let him lug on you." *Similar to when your truck's engine "lugs" just before it stalls. When you slow down, don't let him slow into a four-beat lope so the judge has to guess whether you are loping or trotting.*

Mauling

"If he's not listening, just maul him a little." *Get your horse's attention by asking for collection—often useful when trying to get him past something that spooks him.*

Out of Texas by truck

"Oh he's just out of Texas by truck, nothing special." *This horse does not have spectacular breeding and probably no resale value.*

Pony lope

"I don't want to see you pony lope those circles!" *Don't go very slowly and lazily around the circles.*

Push-button

"He's just a push-button horse." *Your horse is so easy to control it's as though you just need to push a button (perform the cue) and he'll do whatever you ask.*

Read the gauges

"Let's see what he's like during this class; just read the gauges." *Let your horse tell you how you need to ride him when you show.*

Set up

"Don't over-think the stop, or he may set up on you." *When your horse begins the action of a stop by moving his body into the stop position prior to you asking him to do so.*

The wheels fell off

"Wow, the wheels really fell off during that run!" *You looked like you were doing okay and then suddenly it all went horribly wrong.*

FOCUS ON THE POSITIVE

After each run, focus on three things you did correctly, even if you have to ask someone to help you and they start off with "Well, you didn't fall off." Write these three affirmations in your competition diary (see sidebar, p. 114). While you will also record three areas where you need improvement, you must make sure to keep your focus on the positive while you are at the show and on the trip home. There will be plenty of time to focus on "getting better" at home.

When you are not finished competing and need to make minor adjustments to your game plan while at the show, these positive statements can help you from focusing too much on what *could* go wrong. Errors in the show pen have told you that you have more work ahead of you at home, but at the show you need to focus on having good, positive runs, even if they are not class-winning ones (fig. 16.2).

If you had major issues in the pen, such as your horse kicking out during lead changes, running off with you, bucking, or refusing to stop, you may have to consider schooling through the next run (see p. 111). Your horse's memory relates to his actions and is relatively short. There is a very good chance that his reaction will be the same in your next class, so you will have the chance to reinforce the bad behavior, or the good.

EVALUATION AT HOME

Your run evaluation does not stop at the end of the show. It's when you're at home again that you need to focus on your areas for improvement.

Schedule a ride with your trainer for the week following. Talk about what you think worked and what didn't. Tell your trainer how you feel about the runs you had and where you think you went wrong, even if you think he already knows. As knowledgeable as your trainer may be, he wasn't the one riding your horse, and he can't read your mind.

If you ride without a trainer, it may be a good idea to pick up a few training videos and review them

Karen Davis, Rookie Reiner, Woodinville, Washington, on positive reinforcement:

"Rookies need someone to meet them at the out gate who can tell them the good things about their run. We 'feel' our scores, know all the things we did wrong, and are very hard on ourselves because we want to succeed. We can rarely pick out the things we did well."

16.2   At the end of your run, take a moment to breathe and focus on the positive.

between shows. The key is to make a list of problem areas and watch for tips specific to that area.

MOST COMMON ROOKIE MISTAKES

Overpracticing

According to trainer Roberta McCarty, the most common mistake for rookies (and even for some higher level Non Pros) outside the show pen is overpracticing. "They don't understand what effect practicing has on their horses." What it can do is reinforce small, incorrect actions until they become ingrained in both horse and rider. The rider doesn't mean to make the mistake over and over again, but because no one is watching, he becomes sloppier. "To learn maneuvers, you must have some repetition, but I think beginners need supervised repetition," she says.

Cory Hutchings concurs that overpracticing or over-riding is one of the top mistakes rookies make. "If a beginner has seen someone else—like her trainer or the previous owner—show her horse to a score of 72, she wants to mark the same, even if she isn't ready yet. My philosophy is that you should go out and get a correct ride first before you try and ride for a higher score. I might show her horse in a class and purposefully mark a 70 to show her that she doesn't have to go all out to mark a score that might easily win the class. I just want a rookie to ride correctly and stay out of the penalty box."

If you feel as if you've been trying to fix a maneuver all day and just can't get it right, then you might be guilty of overpracticing.

Speed

Another common mistake is adding speed in the show pen before either the rider or horse is capable of executing a pattern. Prior to a show, McCarty regularly checks in with her riders to ask how fast they are planning on running their horse in the pen. At first, many reply that they are going to go as fast as they can or that they don't know, but this is a mistake.

"If you don't know how fast you are going to go, how do you know how to practice and prepare at home? You can't show faster than you've been practicing. It's a big surprise to the horse and the result is that the rider loses control of the horse and all sorts of bad things happen. We teach everybody that speed kills and tell them the speed they should be going. So when they go into the show pen, they are riding at the same speed that they were at home and they maintain control."

When your horse starts to speed up without your say-so or if you find yourself thinking "Oh boy, I'm really going fast here!" you might be guilty of speed violations.

Going too slowly is also a mistake. One of the hardest lessons for a rookie to learn is to "run the horse to the stop," which is making sure the horse is running at peak speed just before you say, "Whoa." Maintaining a consistent increase in speed is crucial to a proper run-down and sliding stop, and forgetting to do it, or allowing the horse to dictate the speed are commonly seen.

"It's very tricky to get the right amount of 'run and stop' without getting too much 'run' or too much 'stop,'" says McCarty. "This happens a lot when a beginner is riding an older horse that has been shown a lot. Instead of the rookie making the decision about the run, the horse makes it for her and she ends up being a passenger rather than the conductor. There's also timing (when to ask for the stop) and straightness (of the run to the stop) involved in this maneuver. It seems like it should be simple, but it's not."

When your horse tells you that it's time to stop, or he doesn't slide very far when he does stop, you might be going too slowly.

To make matters worse, according to McCarty and many other seasoned competitors, the more you practice stopping the worse the horse runs. The horse may become tired or start to anticipate the cue while the rider is seeking "just one more good stop" before she gets off.

Video Recommendations

How to Train and Maintain Your Own Reining Horse by Greenridge Productions

Reining Fundamentals by Al Dunning

Reining to Win by Dell Hendricks

Improving Your Score by Good as Gold Reining

Quick Trips to the Penalty Box

Some of the most common rookie penalties are:

Missing the marker when the pattern calls for a stop past a specific one.

Overspinning because you are going too fast.

Missed or late lead changes due to ineffective cues.

Over-cueing a horse and causing him to kick out.

Craig Sutter, NRHA Judge and Non Pro competitor, on "plussing":

"In order to win, I think most rookies attempt to overshow their entire pattern and end up failing. Attempting to mark a 75 by 'plussing' every maneuver usually results in a score closer to a 65. Our scoring system is very specific. Successful riders understand the scoring system and make a plan according to what their horse is able to accomplish: 'Show what you have.' If your horse has +1/2 spins, you could be marked a 71 if you were able to +1/2 both spins and then 'zero' the remaining maneuvers while staying out of the penalty box. A 71 will win a lot of rookie reining classes! By focusing on what your horse *can* do and how the patterns are segmented into maneuvers, you can show your horse to the best of his ability."

17 *Freestyle Reining*

Pounding music, clapping crowds, and standing ovations: all these characterize some of the best freestyle reining performances the industry sees. Created to draw in the audience, attract newcomers, and rev up the crowd during Saturday night performances, freestyle reining has its own rules and own section of the judging handbook.

HOW "FREESTYLE" IS FREESTYLE

According to the *NRHA Handbook*, freestyle reining, "not only provides an opportunity to use these maneuvers creatively, but also to expand them to music by means of choreography. Riders are encouraged to use musical scores, which permit them to show the athletic ability of the horse in a crowd-appealing way."

There are several required maneuvers that must be included: a minimum of four consecutive spins to the left, four consecutive spins to the right, three stops, one lead change at the lope from left to right, one lead change at the lope from right to left. Notice that there is no requirement for circles, but you should use as much of the pen as possible.

THE BENEFITS OF FREESTYLE

If you are looking to build confidence in yourself and your horse, a freestyle class might be an excellent option. The defined parameters allow you to capitalize on your horse's strengths and downplay his weaknesses. If your horse's strength is his stop and his weakness is his spin, you only need to do the required number of spins and can do a few extra stops for effect.

Stacy Westfall of Mount Gilead, Ohio, multiple-time winner of NRHA Freestyle reining competitions, is well-known for her freestyle performances both bridle-less and bareback. "The biggest misconception about freestyle reining is that people automatically think that the artistic component is the primary focus," says Westfall. "They lose sight of the fact that it's still reining and that the maneuvers need to be just as strong because it's still scored like regular reining but with the addition of credit for artistic impression."

To make the most of your first freestyle, Westfall suggests entering a local show before moving on to larger events. However, do go watch larger events such as the Quarter Horse Congress or the NRHA Futurity where the crowd is positively electric.

ESSENTIAL MUSIC TIPS

When beginning to design a new freestyle pattern, Westfall takes her horse's personality and movement into consideration. One of the first freestyles Westfall performed was originally going to be to the song "Desperado" by the Eagles—she'd picked it out long before she actually began planning to ride to it.

"I just pictured a dark horse and a duster and a bandana," she says. "The whole thing came to my mind instantly. But when I was finally in a position to realize the dream of competing in a big class, I had a mare named Can Can Lena and she was a choppy kind of mover whereas 'Desperado' is a very slow, flowing kind of a song, and I couldn't get it to work in my head because I knew the horse's movement wouldn't fit the song." Fortunately the mare's owner suggested the Johnny Cash song, "Ghost Riders in the Sky," and Westfall could hear the rhythm in her head instantly. "I knew I had the right song for that horse." She kept the same costume and theme as her original concept, and it fit the mare's serious personality. (This video is available on www.YouTube.com and has been viewed over 300,000 times.)

Westfall avoids currently popular songs, which are more likely to be used by other riders. For example, when Big and Rich came out with their song "Save a Horse, Ride a Cowboy," she heard it at every freestyle she attended.

Westfall listens to her freestyle music over and over to avoid becoming emotional about the song. This prevents her from overriding her horse during the event (see sidebar). However, she doesn't over-practice the pattern she's designed in order to prevent her horse from "anticipating" maneuvers. Instead, she uses a good MP3 player during general warm-ups to practice her timing and get an idea of just how much of the arena she needs to use. This means that her pattern may change slightly from location to location.

"During open riding (when anyone is allowed to warm up in the arena), if my first set of maneuvers is to trot in and spin both directions, I'll hit play as I enter and do just that, then hit pause. I'll look at how much time it took me. My horse doesn't know I was listening to the music and doesn't know what's coming next. Then I'll look around the arena and decide where my next maneuver can be. I stand there and I wait until the timing is right, working around all the other riders. I press play again, do my next sequence and hit pause again, repeating this so I can get my timing down in the arena without burning my horse out."

17.1 Freestyle patterns should have an artistic theme but not overlook the technical aspects.

#1 Freestyle Mistake

Most new freestyle riders override their horses in the pen. They get caught up in the music, ask a lot more than the horse is capable of doing, and end up showing the judge what they *can't* do instead of what they *can.*

Clear Clothing Choices

A costume is not actually an essential piece of a freestyle pattern, though traditionally one is worn. Technically, freestyle is simply an artistically run pattern set to music. Westfall suggests picking a song that has a clear theme so that you can pick an outfit to match. Don't make your audience guess what your theme is—make it simple.

17.2 *The possibilities of your freelance reining program are practically limitless. Multiple-time NRHA Freestyle winner Stacy Westfall is known for her bridleless—and sometimes bareback—performances.*

The Problem with Going Bridleless

A new phenomenon is to perform freestyle without a bridle—something popularized by Westfall herself. But she cautions riders from attempting this before they are ready.

"I think the only problem with going bridleless is that riders have gotten obsessed with it to the point of thinking it covers all flaws—the judge is going to be 'wowed' and you can pretend that mistakes aren't happening. I see people taking bridles off horses when they don't have any right to do so. Riders think that they have control but they're not really there yet. You can have fun with freestyle, but only if you are safe."

Choose music that has varying tempos and crescendos. You can use these parts to highlight your speed transitions and stops. Or, you can speed up and slow down a spin. However, don't get too caught up with making the maneuvers time perfectly to the music.

"I want to match my maneuvers to the music but not to the point of obsessing about it. I plan more dramatic maneuvers like flying changes and spins when the music is 'up.' I don't need to time every step," says Westfall. "I don't try to hit specific notes because you end up 'setting up' your body and telegraphing the next maneuver to your horse, who just goes ahead and does it. Plus, you'll get very frustrated trying to time music with maneuvers. You'll be pleasantly surprised by how many people come out and say 'your timing was so perfect in that one spot' and you can smile and nod. Nobody will say, 'You know, if you had hit that stop two notes earlier...'"

Choose music that fits to a three-and-a-half-minute time limit so you don't have to worry about making your run fit. If you are creating your own music with a mix of songs, make sure it sounds professional. If your music has poor transitions and sounds as though it's been taken off the radio, the impression you leave will not be positive.

SCORING

In a freestyle run, the maneuver scores carry more weight than the overall artistic score, so freestyle is not a free-for-all to see how creative you can be while letting the correctness of your maneuvers suffer. The artistic impression judge or the commonly used "applause-meter" technique cannot represent more than 20 percent of the combined score.

You can include non-classical reining maneuvers such as half-passes and side-passes, turns on the forehand, and trotting. If you include additional reining maneuvers above the required number, you do not get additional maneuver marks, but their scores will serve to increase or decrease existing scores already given for the required maneuvers. In other words, once you have completed a lead change in each direction you may include others and if they are all good, you may keep the higher maneuver score. But if they start becoming worse (or incorrect) then your overall lead-change mark will drop.

There is some leeway in the rules for equipment that is normally not allowed, provided that it is "non-abusive and humane." For example, joined English reins (have no tail and are attached to one another with a buckle) are allowed in freestyle, but not in regular reining classes.

You will only be judged while astride your horse and you may use props, though they will not add to your score. At no time can the prop hinder the judges' view of the horse.

Because of the difficulty judging a freestyle class, three judges are used with one of them deemed to be the "tie-break judge." When there is a tie, the technical merit scores of that judge will be used to decide the winner.

CHOREOGRAPHY TIPS

Know how long it will take your horse to perform the required maneuvers. It isn't an exact science since you won't have to worry about making your maneuvers occur at specific areas in the pen, like the usual changes at center or stop past the marker. You can adjust the distances to accommodate smaller or larger arenas. Try to be symmetrical and use all of the arena space that you can. Don't let your pattern look as if you are just winging it–practice ahead of time and learn the lyrics so that you can remember which maneuver they correspond with.

Westfall suggests using the choreography to show the best parts of your horse. "Know your horse. If you've got a really big 'stopper' then do a few extra stops. If you have a weak turner, don't throw in an extra set of spins at the end. If you've got a horse that circles really well, do the circles even though they aren't called for in the required maneuvers and if you have a horse that doesn't circle well, just leave them out. Freestyle gives you the opportunity to make positive decisions about showing off your horse."

PLAN AND PRACTICE

You may not have access to a sound system at home, but riding with a set of headphones and a CD or MP3 player can work just as well since your horse does not need to hear the music. When practicing, experiment

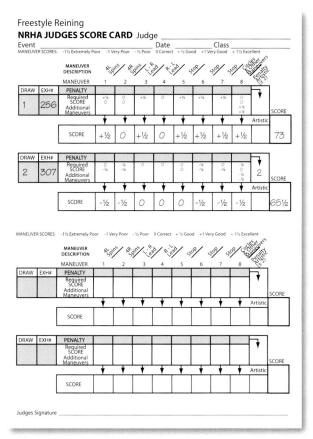

17.3   The judge's score sheet for freestyle reining has more room for scores than the standard score sheet (see fig. 8.2, p. 56) and can test a scribe's addition and subtraction skills.

with different maneuvers during any refrains in the music so you have a ready-made plan to substitute if you arrive to find that the show does not have good ground or your horse suddenly develops an issue with a specific maneuver.

Try to have at least one practice run prior to your class. Most show committees offer freestyle practice times, knowing that it can be difficult to coordinate music and costumes. When you deliver your music to the sound or announcer's booth, clearly label it with instructions to avoid confusion. Even better, have one song only on the CD by making a copy or burning a CD for this specific purpose. By having instructions such as, "Fast forward to one minute, eight seconds, and press 'play' as soon as I stand at center and nod my head," you increase the likelihood of human error in the sound booth. Better to have simpler instructions, such as "Press 'play' when I enter."

When planning your pattern, keep in mind that required maneuvers have priority. When Westfall maps out her ride, she keeps the required patterns in the forefront of her thoughts and thinks about which extra maneuvers she could add in. "If I enter a pen and I feel as if I'm running out of time, then the first thing I start cutting is the optional maneuvers, which might affect your artistic score a little bit, but you have to get the required maneuvers in or none of the rest matters," she says. "If you're really nervous, I suggest putting in your required maneuvers early so that you get them out of the way—then you've got a little less stress at the end."

Westfall has always kept her freestyle patterns simple but stylish. She doesn't overdo one maneuver or another. "If you do four flying lead changes and you're only required to do two, and on your third you drag a lead, you still get a penalty. I always encourage people to do the best they can and minimize the potential for error. One of my least favorite things is seeing someone running up and down the arena almost looking out of control, doing 10 slides. An uneducated crowd will love it because it's exciting and fast, but the judges don't because it loses the 'willingly guided or controlled with the no apparent resistance and dictated to completely' look."

By thinking ahead of time and focusing on the basics of reining: maintaining control, precision, and correctness, you can avoid mistakes and experience more success. As Westfall cautions, "By planning ahead, you're a lot less likely to do something that leaves you saying 'Why did I try to throw that extra slide in? Why did I try to do that?'"

18 Planning Your Reining Future

To best judge your growth as a competitor, look at your reining career as if it is a real career. Long-term planning and goal-setting will help keep your success steady and manageable. Previous chapters have included important information like staying in lower-level classes and moving up only when you are ready. So how do you know it's time?

STEPPING UP

Each level of approved classes uses rider earnings to determine where you show. This structure assumes that you are improving with each dollar you earn and helps to ensure that riders are challenged to do better by eventually requiring them to ride against stiffer competition.

When it is time to step up and out of the beginner classes, you should have a game plan that includes additional training on your horse. You should be at a point in your reining career where a good run is not an accident, but something that is planned.

UPGRADING YOUR MOUNT

It can be sad to say goodbye to your rookie-level horse. This horse has carried you through nerve-wracking times, forgiven your mistakes, and been patient with new training techniques. But sometimes this horse isn't competitive enough for the higher levels.

You will know it is time to "upgrade" when you are consistently achieving the same scores and not making the common mental mistakes that used to result in penalties, says Cory Hutchings. "When my rookies come out of the pen with the same average score they got at the last few shows and ask what they did wrong and I can honestly say 'nothing, you rode perfectly,' then they know it's time to upgrade to a horse that can take them as far as they want to go."

You have two choices. You can ride the same horse and try to make him—and you—better. Or, you can move on to a different horse that is already more competitive and work on improving your riding to meet his ability. It is always less frustrating for a rookie to ride a horse that is just a little bit better than he is. When the opposite occurs and your ability exceeds your horse's, you feel as if you are being prevented from achieving the scores you want.

Perhaps you could pass your rookie horse on to a family member. Or, he could go on to help another rookie achieve the same level of success. One thing is certain: there is—and always will be—a market for good, broke, rookie-level reining horses.

Buying a new horse for yourself as you move up in class levels is very similar to buying a rookie horse as

Reiner John Milchick, of Boston, Kentucky, on "slowing down":

"The hardest lesson for me to learn was (and still is) to *slow down*. And by that I mean, slow down:

"My hands so they are easier on the horse's mouth, asking softly before demanding.

"The day's training and not try to do everything in one day (it's way too hard on the horse).

"The speed and not ask the horse for more than he is ready to do.

"In the show pen and not rushing from one element to the next.

"My breathing and my brain in the show pen, focusing on one element at a time.

"By nature, I am a Type A personality and control freak (lots of reiners are, I've discovered), and so I want to go charging ahead. And reining—more than anything else that I've ever done—takes time and patience."

Trainer Mario Boisjoli on how everyone could use a better horse:

"*I could use a better horse! You can always upgrade.*"

I discussed it in chapter 4 (p. 22). Except now, you can take a more active role in riding and choosing the prospect, and you might consider getting a younger horse.

The purpose of upgrading isn't to find a horse to "use" for a couple of years. It is to search for your new partner.

TRANSITIONING TO A NEW TRAINER

The trainer and client relationship is a symbiotic one that depends on both sides of the team giving 100-percent commitment and dedication to the showing of

your horse. If you find a trainer who is able to partner with you and help you show, it is important to discuss mutual expectations.

Sometimes, good relationships sour or cease to work on both sides. In most cases, this isn't a matter of one person doing something wrong, but caused instead by a miscommunication of goals and desires at the outset of the relationship and/or a failure to adjust as needs change. Some areas where this happens between a trainer and a Non Pro may include:

▶ Time commitment at shows

▶ Number of weekly lessons, whether private or group

▶ Number of times the trainer rides the horse each week or month

▶ Communication or teaching style

▶ Level of care for the horse

▶ Amount of advice and guidance needed with decision-making and goals

As a rookie, you may feel a little insecure about how to establish a relationship with a trainer. How do you know how much attention you need at a show if you've never been to one? In addition to the section on choosing a trainer from chapter 2 (p. 12) , you also need to determine what your "deal breakers" are. What types of behavior can you absolutely not tolerate from your trainer? Items such as animal abuse and dishonesty, of course, will be at the top of your list. And, make sure you know what your trainer will not tolerate from you: for example, failing to pay your bills on time, or disrespecting his time and energy by not showing up for scheduled lessons.

But some reasons for a relationship breakup are not as clear cut as the ones I've outlined. For example, you may not be seeing the results you hoped for, despite holding up your end of the bargain (showing up on time for lessons, having your horse in training, and keeping to time and financial commitments). Perhaps the trainer's barn has changed its focus a bit and whereas you were once one of the only Non Pros there, you are now surrounded by youth riders.

First, it is okay to change trainers. But, you don't want to get into the habit of "trainer hopping" (moving from one trainer to another without giving each new trainer a chance to help). So, barring any abuse or dishonesty issues, you should finish out your show year with the trainer you started with to ensure your commitments are met.

Plan to approach your trainer and tell him the arrangement is not working for you any longer and at this point, you can renegotiate the terms of your relationship or decide on a date to move your horse and sever the client-trainer relationship officially. It is best to have this discussion before you have made a commitment to another trainer. Your trainer should not be offended to be told that his program is not working for you—no one program works for every Non Pro. He may even be willing to suggest a trainer that might be better suited to your style of learning.

Remember, each run, each show, each horse you ride can take you a step ahead or a step back—but no matter what, keep looking forward, learning, and growing as a reining competitor.

18.1 *You must develop an open relationship with your trainer so that you can discuss issues that arise in your first year of showing.*

Biographies of Featured Reiners and Trainers

ROBERTA MCCARTY from Temecula, California, has been training reining horses for over 25 years. In 2006 she was named to the NRHA Top Twenty Professionals list. McCarty is a two-term past President of the California Reining Horse Association (CRHA) and currently serves on its Board of Directors. The McCarty Ranch is well known for its great Non Pro coach program for both beginners and more seasoned Non Pros. McCarty and her husband have taken a competitor to the NRHA Rookie of the Year competition at least eight times. In 2000, McCarty's student Alicia Briquelet and Heir To Shine were crowned Rookie of the Year Champions. McCarty trains with her husband, Jim. You can find them online at www.mccartyranch.com.

CORY HUTCHINGS from Arlington, Washington, has competed in APHA, AQHA, and NRHA horse shows. Hutchings sits down with his clients and works to understand their competition needs and goals. He enjoys working with Open owners, Non-Pros, and Youth riders. As a competitor, Cory has many Top Ten Open Division finishes as well as multiple circuit and year end awards. You can find him online at www.cory-hutchings.com.

BOB LOOMIS is an NRHA Hall of Fame member along with his talented stallion Topsail Whiz. Loomis has been training since 1967 and operating his breeding operation since 1974. He is a former president of the NRHA and has stood some of the industry's biggest names: Topsail Cody, Topsail Whiz, and West Coast Whiz. He is regarded as one of the industry's leading reining horse breeders and, along with author Kathy Kadash, wrote *Reining: The Art of Performance in Horses*. You can find the Loomis Ranch online at www.loomisranch.net.

STACY WESTFALL is one of the most well-known female horse trainers in the business. She was the first woman to win Road to the Horse, a competition that features the use of "natural" horse training methods on unbroken colts over a period of two days. She is becoming increasingly well-known for her Freestyle reining performances. In 2005, Westfall won six key reining events without reins, including runs at Fiesta in the Park, the NRHA Eastern Affiliate Championship, the Tradition Freestyle Open, the Tulsa Reining Classic, the All American Quarter Horse Congress, and a repeat win at the NRHA Futurity. She repeated her Tulsa championship in 2006 without a saddle or bridle. You can find Westfall online at www.westfallhorsemanship.com.

BARBRA SCHULTE is a cutting horse trainer, international clinician, and author. She is a gifted teacher and brings this talent to her clients through her Mentally Tough® program. Schulte trains recreational and competitive riders from the inside out. She is a Personal Performance Coach, certified by LGE Sports Science, a world leader in personal performance training. Schulte pioneered the integration of personal performance training into the equestrian world. You can find her online at www.barbraschulte.com.

WARWICK SCHILLER began riding and showing horses in 1976, and was drawn toward the Quarter Horse and the Western style of riding. He showed as a youth winning a number of Australian titles. After working in the corporate world, Schiller moved to the United States and worked for AQHA World Champion Don Murphy, flourishing under his mentor's exceptional training. As a professional horse trainer for more than 16 years, Schiller has enjoyed a very successful career. He has trained and shown horses and coached riders to NRHA World Champion and Reserve World Champion titles, as well as Champion and Reserve Champion wins at all of the major reining shows across the United States, including the NRHA Futurity, NRHA Derby, National Reining Breeders Classic (NRBC), All American Quarter Horse Congress, Firecracker Classic, Texas Classic, West Coast Spectacular, Reining by the Bay, Hollywood Charity Reining, and the California Reining Challenge. You can find Schiller online at www.schillerquarterhorses.com.

ROBYN SCHILLER rode horses with her mom before she could walk on her own, and she began her show career at the age of five. She began reining in 1996. She won the NRHA Rookie of the Year title in 2001. In 2002, she became one of Warwick Schiller's assistant trainers (she is now married to him) and in 2003 won the NRHA Limited Open World Championship and the Intermediate Open Reserve World Championship. Schiller has competed at all major NRHA events in the United States, including the USET Festival of Champions. She received her NRHA judge's card in 2006. Schiller is also on Reining Australia's Board of Directors. You can find her online at www.schillerquarterhorses.com.

SHAWNA SAPERGIA was born into one of Canada's top reining families and has been riding since childhood. Her father, Vern, and her mother, Molly, helped guide her toward success by instilling a strong work ethic and a dedication to equine athletes. Sapergia began competing on the Quarter Horse circuits across Canada in a variety of disciplines from trail and barrels to Western pleasure and showmanship. One particular event drew her attention and as she entered young adulthood, she began to focus solely on the sport of reining. The athleticism and finesse of the reining horse appealed to Sapergia and soon after high school, the young trainer began to make her mark on the Canadian reining scene. To date, she has surpassed $100,000 NRHA earnings and has been one of the longest standing Reining Team Canada members, having qualified for the team in 2001, 2002, and 2006. In 2006 she was the NRHA Intermediate Open Futurity Champion. You can find her online at www.sapergiareiners.com.

Appendix I

SAMPLE COMPETITION DIARY

Keeping track of your scores over the course of a show season can provide invaluable data, telling you where you are getting better and what you still need to improve. I recommend creating your own in a simple format, such as this:

Show:
Date:
Class:
# of competitors:
Score:
Placing:
Earnings (this class):
Earnings (to date):

Maneuver scores and penalties:

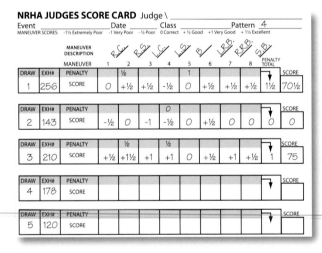

Three things that I did right:

1

2

3

Three areas to work on:

1

2

3

Appendix II

RULES FOR JUDGING

(Note: these penalties were taken from the 2007 *NRHA Handbook* and may have changed—consult your most up-to-date version of the rule book.)

▶ A judge is required to penalize a horse ½ point for a delayed change of lead by one stride where the lead change is required by the pattern description.

▶ Deduct ½ point for starting circle at a jog or exiting rollbacks at a jog up to two strides.

▶ Jogging behind two strides but less than half circle or half length of the arena, deduct 2 points.

▶ Deduct ½ point for over- or underspinning up to an eight of a turn; deduct 1 point for over- or underspinning up to a quarter of a turn.

▶ In patterns requiring a runaround, failure to be on the correct lead when rounding the end of the arena will be penalized as follows: for half the turn or less, 1 point; for more than half the turn, 2 points.

▶ There will be a ½ point penalty for failure to remain a minimum of 20 feet from the wall or fence when approaching a stop and/or rollback.

1-Point Penalties

Each time a horse is out of lead or has a delayed change of lead, a judge is required to penalize by 1 point. The penalty for being out of lead is cumulative and the judge will add 1 penalty point for each quarter of the circumference of a circle or any part thereof that a horse is out of lead. A delayed change of lead is a 1 point penalty from one stride to a quarter of the circumference of a circle and is also cumulative beyond that point (see fig. I A).

2-Point Penalties

▶ Break of gait.

▶ "Freezing up" in spins or rollbacks.

▶ On walk-in patterns, cantering prior to reaching the center of the arena and/or failure to stop or walk before executing a canter departure.

▶ On run-in patterns, failure to be in a canter prior to reaching the first marker.

▶ If a horse does not completely pass the specified marker before initiating a stop position.

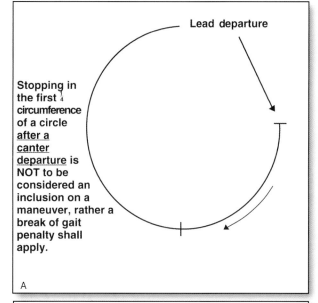

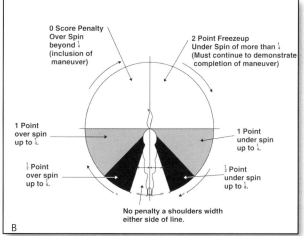

I A & B   The NRHA has specific guidelines for how to penalize improper lead departures (A) and overspins (B).

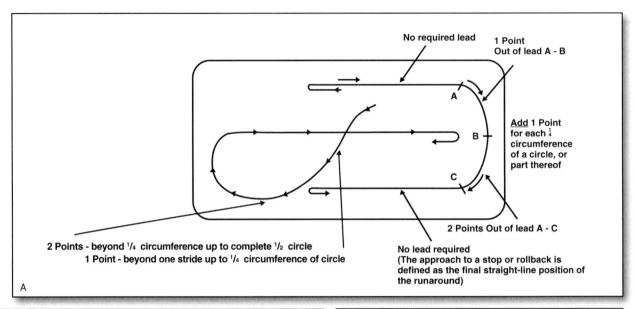

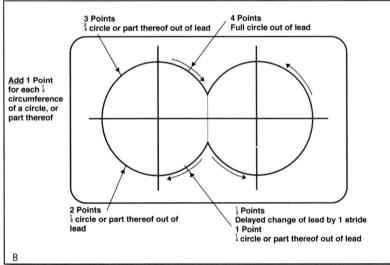

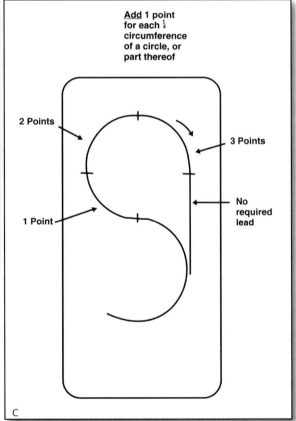

II A–C   *Penalties for being out of lead in runarounds (A),
during changes (B), or partial circles and rundowns (C).*

All penalty illustrations are used courtesy of the NRHA.

5-Point Penalties

► Spurring in front of cinch.
► Use of either hand to instill fear or praise.
► Holding saddle with either hand.
► Blatant disobedience including kicking, biting, bucking, rearing, and striking.

"Zero" Scores

► Use of more than index or first finger between reins.
► Use of two hands (exception in snaffle bit or hackamore classes designated for two hands) or changing hands.
► Use of romal other than as outlined in Rules for

III   There are also penalties calculated for jogging during your pattern.

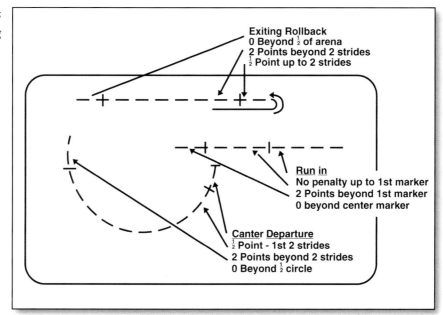

Judging B.5 (see your copy of the *NRHA Handbook*).

▶ Failure to complete pattern as written.

▶ Performing the maneuvers other than in specified order.

▶ The inclusion of maneuvers not specified, including, but not limited to 1) backing more than two strides, 2) turning more than 90 degrees (Exception: a complete stop in the first quarter of a circle after a canter departure is not considered an inclusion of maneuver; a 2-point break of gait penalty will apply).

▶ Equipment failure that delays completion of pattern.

▶ Balking or refusal of command where performance is delayed.

▶ Running away or failing to guide where it becomes impossible to discern whether the entry is on pattern.

▶ Jogging in excess of one-half circle or one-half length of the arena.

▶ Overspins of more than a quarter turn.

▶ Fall to the ground by horse or rider (a horse is deemed to have fallen when his shoulder and/or hip and/or underline touches the ground).

▶ Dropping a rein that contacts the ground while the horse is in motion.

▶ Failure to wear appropriate Western attire as outlined in the *NRHA Handbook* (see chapter 6, p. 44).

No Scores

▶ Infraction of any state or federal law, which exists pertaining to the exhibition, care, and custody of horses within the state or country where an NRHA reining is being held.

▶ Abuse of an animal in the show arena and/or evidence that an act of abuse has occurred prior to or during the exhibition of a horse in competition.

▶ Use of illegal equipment, including wire on bits, bosals, or curb chains.

▶ Use of illegal bits, bosals, or curb chains.

▶ Use of tack collars, tie downs, or nose bands.

▶ Use of whips or bats.

▶ Use of any attachment that alters the movement or circulation to the tail.

▶ Failure to dismount and/or present horse and equipment to the appropriate judge for inspection.

▶ Disrespect or misconduct by the exhibitor.

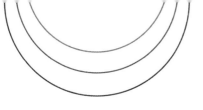

Appendix III

AFFILIATES AND NATIONAL AFFILIATES

Affiliates
For information about the NRHA Affiliate Program, see chapter 1, p. 5.

National Association Affiliates (NAA)
Each country that participates in the NRHA's International Affiliate Program (IAP) has its own National Association Affiliate (NAA) that has met the conditions outlined in NRHA bylaws, applied for NAA status, and has been approved by the NRHA. The NAA is then recognized by the NRHA as the organization to provide governance and leadership for the sport of reining on a national level in its country. The NAA is responsible for promoting reining within its own country, choosing its international team, and serving its national membership. Individual competitors pay their membership directly to the NRHA, but a portion of that membership is rebated back to the NAA to help implement programs in its own country. The NAA uses the *NRHA Handbook* and NRHA-accredited judges. There can only be one NAA in a country and to be approved it must have 25 members in good standing with the NRHA. There must be a minimum of four NRHA-approved shows each year and the NAA must submit reports on past and future activities. The NAA may not host reining shows and may only provide administrative support and program development to the affiliates in its country.

Contact Information for the NRHA, Affiliates, and National Affiliates

National Reining Horse Association
3000 NW 10th Street
Oklahoma City, OK 73107
Ph: 405.946.7400
Fax: 405.946.8425
www.nrha.com

NRHA Affiliates: Breeds

Appaloosa Reining Horse Association
www.aprha.com

National Morgan Reining Horse Association
www.nmrha.com

NRHA Affiliates: By State and Country

MOUNTAIN US

Central Plains Reining Horse Association
www.cprha.com

Cowboy States Reining Horse Association
www.cowboystatesreiners.com

Eastern Plains Reining Horse Association
www.eprha.org

Intermountain Reining Horse Association
www.irha.com

Montana Reining Horse Association
http://mtrha.com

Northern Rockies Reining Horse Association
www.northernrockiesreining.com

Rocky Mountain Reining Horse Association
www.rmrha.com

Western Slope Reining Horse Association
www.wsrha.com

Yellowstone Reining Horse Association
www.yellowstonereining.com

NORTH CENTRAL US

Illinois Reining Horse Association
www.ilrhanews.com

Indiana Reining Horse Association
www.inrha.org

Midwest Reining Horse Association
www.mwrha.com

North Central Reining Horse Association
www.ncrha.com

NORTHEASTERN US

Central Kentucky Reining Horse Association
www.ckrha.org

Central New York Reining Horse Association
www.cnyrha.com

Central Ohio Reining Horse Association
www.centralohioreining.com

East Coast Reiners Association
www.ecraonline.com

Eastern Pennsylvania Reining Horse Association
www.eprha.com

Michigan Reining Horse Association
www.mrha.org

Northeast Reining Horse Association
www.nerha.com

Ohio Valley Reining Horse Association
www.ovrha.com

Tri-State Reining Horse Association

Virginia Reining Horse Association
www.virginiareininghorse.com

Yankee Reining Horse Association
www.yankeereiners.com

NORTHWESTERN US

Idaho Reining Horse Association
www.idahoreining.com

Northwest Reining Horse Association
www.nwraonline.net

Oregon Reining Horse Association
www.oregonreining.com

Reining Horse Association of the Northwest
www.rhanw.com

Snake River Reining Alliance
www.snakeriverreining.com

Washington Reining Horse Association
www.wrha.net

West Coast Reining Horse Association
www.wcrha.com

SOUTH CENTRAL US

Four States Reining Horse Association

Heart of Texas Reining Horse Association
www.hotrha.net

Kansas Reining Horse Association
www.kansasreining.com

Louisiana Reining Horse Association
www.thelrha.com

Missouri Reining Horse Association
www.mrha-reiners.com

Oklahoma Reining Horse Association
www.okrha.com

Southwest Missouri Reining Horse Association
www.smrha.net

Southwest Reining Horse Association
www.swrha.com

Texas Reining Horse Association
www.trhaonline.com

West Texas Reining Horse Association
www.wtrha.com

SOUTHEASTERN US

Alabama Reining Horse Association
www.alrha.org

Dixie Reining Horse Association

Florida Reining Horse Association
www.frha.com

Mississippi Reining Horse Association
www.msrha.com

South Florida Reining Horse Association
www.sfrha.com

Southeastern Reining Horse Association
www.serha.info

Tennessee Reining Horse Association
www.tnrha.org

SOUTHWESTERN US

Arizona Reining Horse Association
www.azrha.com

California Reining Horse Association
www.calreining.com

Central Coast Reining Horse Association
www.ccrha.org

Desert Reining Horse Association
www.desertrha.com

New Mexico Reining Horse Association
www.nmrha.org

Southern Nevada Reining Horse Association
www.lvspinclassic.com

EASTERN CANADA

New Brunswick Codiac Reining Horse Association
http://nbcra.blogspot.com/

Ontario Reining Horse Association
www.orha.on.ca

Association Québécoise de Reining
www.reining.qc.ca

WESTERN CANADA

Central Canada Reining Horse Association
www.ccrha.com

Prince George Reining Horse Association
www.prgrha.com

Reining Alberta
www.reiningalberta.net

Reining Canada (NAA)
www.reiningcanada.com

Saskatchewan Reining Horse Association
www.saskreining.com

Western Canadian Reining Association
www.wrca.info

EUROPE

British Reining (NAA)
www.britishreining.co.uk

Dutch Reining (NAA)
www.drha.nl

Italian Reining Horse Association (NAA)
www.itrha.com

NRHA Belgium (NAA)
www.nrha.be

NRHA Czech (NAA)
www.nrha.cz

NRHA Austria (NAA)
www.nrha-austria.at

NRHA Denmark
www.nrha.dk

NRHA Finland
www.nrha.fi

NRHA of France (NAA)
www.nrha.fr

NRHA Switzerland (NAA)
www.nrha.ch

Reiners of Luxembourg

Reining Deutschland (NAA)
www.reining-deutschland.de

Scandinavian Reining Horse Association (NAA)
www.srha.nu

Spanish Reining Horse Association

SOUTH AMERICA

Asociacion Noreste de Caballo de Reining
www.anecr.com

ANCR Brazil (NAA)
www.ancr.org.br

Caballos de Rienda del Bajio

CARIBBEAN

Asociacion Dominicana de Reining

AUSTRALIA

ACT & Southern NSW Country RHA

Goulburn Valley Reining Horse Association
www.gvrha.com

NSW Reining Horse Association
www.reiningnsw.com

Queensland Reining Horse Association
www.qrha.org.au

Reining Australia (NAA)
www.reiningaustralia.com.au

Southern Queensland Reining Horse Association
www.sqrha.org.au

Victorian Reining Horse Association
www.vrha.com.au

ASIA

NRHA Japan

MIDEAST

NRHA Israel (NAA)

Acknowledgments

Thank you to Craig Sutter, NRHA Judge, for answering all my judging questions, even dumb ones. And to the wonderful, opinionated, and passionate members of the Reining For Fun group (online at sports.groups.yahoo. com/group/ReiningForFun), especially Karen Shedlauskas, Jeanine Kern, Kristy and John Milchick, Kelsey Davis, and of course, (the late and beautiful) Karen Davis.

There were many industry members who lent me their time—if their name appears in this book, know that I'm grateful for their patience and support. I'd also like to mention Kevin Pole, Dave Young, and Bob and Jason Grimshaw, all of whom coached me at one time or another. You were there through hours in the saddle during winters so cold I couldn't feel my toes (climbing on two-year-old colts feeling like the Stay Puft Marshmallow Man) and summer show days where I would collapse hot and exhausted on a hay bale. I can still hear your words of encouragement echoing in my head. I wish every rookie could start with such excellent guidance.

Photo & Illustration Credits

PHOTO CREDITS

Heather Cook: pp. 3, 4, 5, 8, 29, 30, 31, 32, 33, 35, 36, 37, 38, 41, 42, 43, 46 (*bottom left*), 49 (*middle*), 50, 58, 60, 61, 62, 63, 64, 65, 66, 73, 75, 95, 97, 100, 101, 114

Cheryl James: pp. 6, 71

Waltenberry: pp. 7, 45, 46 (*top left*), 49 (*top, bottom*), 116, 119, 120

Geri Greenall: pp. 13, 14, 125

Charlotte Robinson: p. 16

Darrell Dodds: p. 18 (*top left, top right, bottom left*)

Robb Walther: p. 18 (*bottom right*)

Michael Gonzalez: p. 40

Courtesy of Hobby Horse Clothing Company: pp. 46 (*top middle left, top middle right, top right, bottom right*), 47, 48 (*left*)

Courtesy of Girletz Gear: p. 48 (*right*)

Courtesy of the NRHA: pp. 39, 56, 77, 78, 79, 80, 81, 82, 83, 91, 108, 121, *Appendices*

ILLUSTRATION CREDITS

Sandra Scherger: pp. 16, 19, 29, 38, 68, 69, 71, 74

Steve Schiestel: pp. 56, 70, 95, 98, 103, 104

Index

Page numbers in *italics* indicate illustrations.